THE LIFE OF
ST AUGUSTINE

THE LIFE OF ST AUGUSTINE

F.W. Farrar, DD, FRS

Edited by Robert Backhouse

Hodder & Stoughton
LONDON SYDNEY AUCKLAND

British Library Cataloguing in Publication Data.
A catalogue record for this book is available from the British Library.

ISBN 0–340–57773–8

Published by Hodder and Stoughton, a division of Hodder and Stoughton Ltd, Mill Road, Dunton Green, Sevenoaks, Kent TN13 2YA. Editorial Office: 47 Bedford Square, London WC1B 3DP.

Typeset by Watermark, Norfolk House, Hamilton Road, Cromer, Norfolk.

Printed in Great Britain by Cox & Wyman Ltd, Reading, Berks.

Contents

Editor's Introduction

This biography of Augustine is taken from *Lives of the Fathers*, volume 2, which originally had the subtitle 'Sketches of Church History in Biography' and the following quotation by Bishop Wentworth on its title page: 'The History of the Church is represented in certain respects by the history of her great men.' The Rev. Frederic W. Farrar, DD, FRS, was a fellow of Trinity College, Cambridge, Archdeacon of Westminster and Chaplain in Ordinary to the Queen. His book was originally published in 1889 by Adam and Charles Black of Edinburgh. Editorial changes have been kept to a minimum. Much of the Greek, Latin and French found in the footnotes has been omitted. Farrar's list of Augustine's writings has been retained in an appendix.

Farrar was particularly well equipped to write a biography on Augustine. He was not only a specialist in writing biographies of Christians, but was familiar with the doctrinal disputes which absorbed so much of Augustine's thinking. While Farrar clearly had enormous respect for Augustine, he does express his own views occasionally when he disagrees with Augustine's theology. In his chapter on the Pelagian controversy Farrar comments: 'If Pelagius almost did away with grace, Augustine . . . almost did away with free will.' Farrar was equally at home when it came to conveying the spiritual dimensions in Augustine's life. This is especially apparent in his chapter on Augustine's conversion.

After the biblical writers, Augustine has probably had more influence on Christian thought than anyone else. Martin Luther, for example, read more of Augustine's writings, after the Bible, than anybody else's. Throughout the centuries Catholics and Protestants have looked to Augustine for spiritual guidance. It is my prayer that this classic biography of Augustine will challenge and encourage Christians today.

Robert Backhouse
Crostwight Hall, 1992

1

Youth and Education

Aurelius Augustinus (the surname Aurelius is given him by his friend Orosius in the dedication of his history) was the greatest of the Western Fathers, and the man who has exercised the deepest influence on the theology of the church. He was born at Tagaste, a municipality in the province of Constantine in southern Numidia, on or near November 13, 354. Tagaste was an obscure town of Africa, not far from Madaura and Hippo. Here he grew up

> A Roman, moulded by that sun and sea
> That lit and laved the infant Hannibal,
> One who with Afric's blood could still combine
> The civic memories of a Roman line.

The names of his parents were Patricius and Monnica. Patricius, who was from Tagaste, was a heathen who did not become a catechumen till 370 when Augustine was seventeen years old, and who died the following year, shortly after he had been baptised. He was a man of violent temper, who until his conversion to Christianity had little or no regard for religion or morality. He cherished an inordinate ambition for the worldly success of his son, and for this purpose he exercised self-denial in order to give to the brilliant boy an education far higher than might have been expected from his very moderate means. When

9

Augustine was a bishop he once told his congregation that they might have expected him to appear in a more splendid robe, but that this would have ill become a poor man like himself, the son of poor parents. Patricius exercised but little influence over his son, and not for good.

Monnica, on the other hand, was a sincere Christian, the daughter of Christian parents, who owed much to the teaching of a pious nurse to whom they had entrusted the care of their infant.

Among other excellent rules, this aged slave-woman, who had nursed Monnica's father before her, had taught the little girls of the family to live very simply and never to drink even water except at table, lest some day they should be tempted to drink too much wine. 'Now,' she said, 'you drink water; but when you grow up and marry you will have the keys of stores and cellars, and will have got into a habit of drinking, and will despise water but will drink wine.' It was the foolish custom of that day, as of ours, for parents to tempt their children to sip wine even when, as was the case with Monnica, they do not like it. She used to do this when she drew the wine from the cask into a jug. But the wine soon created a fatal craving for itself. She took a little more, and every day a little more, until at last she had got into a habit of secretly drinking cups full of unmixed wine. A single maidservant was the confederate of her evil habit, and one day, when a fierce quarrel rose between them, this girl, with bitterest insult, called her a winebibber. This disgraceful taunt acted on the mind of Monnica like a medicine, and from that moment she saw the foulness of the habit and abandoned it.

She was married at an early age to Patricius, and her married life began unhappily, because her mother-in-law had been set against her by the whispering tongues of evil-minded women-servants. But Monnica so completely overcame these prejudices and won the affection of her husband's mother that she spontaneously informed Patricius of the conduct of these mischievous and malignant women. He, according to the fashion of that day, flogged them, and his mother told them henceforth they should always be flogged if they said a word to her against her daughter-in-law.

Young as Monnica was when she married Patricius, her one desire was to win him to faith and holiness by her meek, loving, and faithful behaviour. When he stormed and raged at her in his passionate moods she defended herself only by silence, and waited till he should return to a better mind. In this way she escaped the blows and personal ill-treatment which in that day so many women had to endure at the hands of heathen husbands. Her neighbours, knowing the sort of man to whom she was married, were amazed that she never had the black eyes and bruised body of which they, though married to gentle husbands, so bitterly complained. But Monnica used to tell them that she, on the other hand, had never had to complain of even one day's domestic strife with her husband. The fault, she answered them, lay not so much in their husbands as in their own ungovernable tongues.

In another way also she set to the matrons of Tagaste an honourable example. She was a universal peacemaker. When ladies quarrelled and poured their immeasurable abuse of one another into her ears, instead of repeating it she let it go no farther, and did her best to reconcile the foes. 'I should have thought this a small virtue,' says Augustine, 'if I had not learnt by experience the endless troubles which, when the horrid pestilence of sins is flowing far and wide, are caused by the repetition of the words of angry enemies and by their exaggeration. It is a man's duty to do his best to alleviate human enmities by kindly speech, not to excite and aggravate them by the repetition of slanders.'

Monnica bore to Patricius at least three children—Augustine, Navigius, and a daughter who is not named, who afterwards became the abbess of a community of nuns.

Augustine was born when Monnica was twenty-three years of age, and she at once made him a catechumen, so that even as an infant he was signed with the sign of the cross, and received 'the sacrament of salt'. She had to struggle from the first against the evil example set to Augustine by his father, but she taught him from the earliest years the name of Jesus, and its sweetness lingered in his memory even in his worst excesses. Augustine might have said, as was said by Lord William Russell when he stood on the scaffold, 'I thank God for having given me a religious education; for even when I forgot it most, it still hung about me and gave me checks.'

We may now follow for some years the direct guidance of Augustine himself. He is one of the very few men who, like Dante in his *Purgatorio*, and Bunyan in his *Grace Abounding*, and yet more directly Rousseau—though in a manner widely different from Rousseau's—has left us his *Confessions*. With holy audacity he lays bare to us the history of his thoughts and passions, the secrets of his life and heart. His objects in writing the *Confessions* were manifold. If he at all resembled other men, it must have cost him a bitter pang thus to reveal the sins of his youth; but he thought—and mankind has confirmed his judgement—that it was well for one among so many millions to say what God had done for his soul. He wished to be known as he really was and as he once had been. Of that book he writes to the Count Darius: 'See what I was in myself and by myself. I had destroyed myself; but He who made me remade me. And when you have found me there, pray for me that I may not fail, but may be perfected.' He also wished to stir up others to the love and fear of God as they read what he had done for his soul, and to show us that 'God has made us for himself and that our heart is restless till it rests in him.' He thought too that men—encouraged by reading how God had led a sinner to forsake the error of his way—might be led to say with him, 'Narrow is the home of my soul that thou shouldst come to it; may it be expanded by thee! It is ruinous; restore it. It has much to offend thine eyes; I confess and know it; but who shall cleanse it, or to whom else shall I cry but thee, "Cleanse me, O Lord, from my secret faults; keep back thy servant also from presumptuous sins"?'

Augustine's *Confessions* have often been compared with those of Rousseau, but they only resemble each other in the fact that both of these writers tried to deal honestly with themselves, and to tell without subterfuge the shame of their past lives. In all other respects they are in violent contrast. Rousseau ends by telling us that he has painted himself as he was, and that if anyone thinks of him as an unworthy man he is himself 'a man to smother'. He begins by saying that when the last trumpet sounds he is ready to present himself book in hand before the sovereign Judge, and calling on all men to listen to his confessions, he will challenge anyone living to say, 'I was better than that man.' Augustine, on the other hand, prostrates himself with tears of bitter penitence at the feet of God to implore the mercy in which he trusted, and to thank God for the peace which he had found, when his saviour had given back to him the clean heart and the free spirit. The confessions of Rousseau are the confessions of the natural, impenitent, unregenerate man; the confessions of Augustine are those of the repentant sinner and the forgiven saint.

He begins with his infancy, when first he entered unconsciously on this mortal life or living death. He speaks of his infant smiles, his first arrival at consciousness, the little fits of temper by which he showed so early the taint of inborn sin. Then came his early boyhood and the beginning of his schooldays. His parents were intensely eager that he should learn much, and distinguish himself, and occupy the then admired position of a teacher of rhetoric and pleader at the bar. For thousands of years down to very recent times the human race has been unable to rise above the brutal stupidity of supposing that the best and indeed the only way of teaching is by means of physical torture.

Augustine was a quick and lively boy, but he could not bear
the drudgery of routine, and he freely criticises the thorny
road through which he was forced to pass by those who
from time immemorial have multiplied labour and sorrow
to the sons of Adam. Like Luther, he acutely felt the horror of being incessantly beaten, in spite of the fact that his
parents and elders laughed at him for being so sensitive.
What seemed to them a trivial harm was to him a deadly
evil, and as a little schoolboy it was his daily and passionate
prayer that he might escape the rod. In this endeavour,
however, he did not succeed, for the charms of playing at
ball were far more immediately attractive than the pros-
pect of being scourged was terrifying. Memory and ability
did not, he found, supersede the necessity of diligence; but
when he had once begun a ball game he could not bear to
be defeated. The love of play, the fondness for the
immoral excitement of the theatres and public games, and
the curiosity with which he listened to the tales of mythology, are the chief faults with which he charges his early
boyhood. But he still bore in mind what he had heard
about eternal life, and when he fell seriously ill and
thought that he was about to die, he entreated his mother
that he might receive baptism. A sudden recovery prevented the granting of his wish, and Monnica shared the
unwise and superstitious view of her age that it was unsafe
to confer baptism until the temptations of early manhood
were past.

As a boy he did not love study in spite of the incessant
pressure put upon him by both his parents 'that he might
satiate the insatiable passions for copious emptiness and
ignominious glory'. One great loss which resulted from
this intellectual indolence was his failure to learn Greek. It
would have been of the utmost use to him in his future
theological studies, and as a consequence of his neglect he
had to depend on Jerome and others for translations of
the masterpieces of Greek theology. He could indeed spell
out the meaning of a simple commentary, but he was never

quite at ease with a Greek book, and had much reason to lament his loss. He had to rely on Victorinus for his views of Plato, and on other translators for his knowledge of Greek philosophy. Meanwhile the romantic emotional boy was delighted with Virgil, for he had learnt Latin from his infancy in the easiest and most pleasant way. He was charmed, he says, with the wanderings of 'some Aeneas or other', while he thought nothing of his own, and wept over the death of Dido with a commiseration which was due rather to his own deadness in trespasses and sins. On the other hand, the multiplication table was detestable to him, and 'twice one is two, twice two is four' was an 'odious lilt' in his ears. Even the terror of the rod could not induce him to love the 'most sweet emptiness' of Homer, because he never could get over the difficulties of the language. We see in these confessions the sort of intellect with which we have to deal. The imaginative boy was father to the man. The voluminous fluency of his genius would have been more precious in quality if it had been controlled and strengthened by a training more rigid and mathematical.

Augustine's education was for the most part literary and classical. Gregory of Nazianzus, Basil, and other Fathers were ardent advocates of the custom of training Christian boys in heathen literature. Augustine, on the other hand, looked on it with considerable misgiving. He was inconsistent in this as in many other opinions, but he felt that there is undoubtedly in the literature of heathendom a 'devouring worm'. He distinctly indicates that it has a corrupting effect, and in support of his view he quotes the youth in Terence's *Eunuchus*, who defends his own immoralities by the example of Jupiter. 'I do not,' says Augustine, 'accuse the words which were chosen and precious vessels, but the wine of error which was drunk to us in the words by drunken teachers, and unless we drank we were beaten, nor might we appeal to any sober judge.' When he declaimed he was loudly applauded both by masters and teachers, but whatever might be the exquisiteness of form, he felt that it would have been better for him if his teachers had been less horrified by solecisms and more by moral faults. The boy's character did not improve. When he shirked his work in order to amuse himself at games or shows, he used to deceive his tutor and his masters and his parents 'by innumerable lies'. He also stole from their table or larder either to indulge his own appetite or to give to his companions. In his games he used to cheat in order to win the victory, although he used furiously to inveigh against his companions when they did the same. When he was caught he used to fly into a passion. And in these faults of boyhood he saw but a prophecy of the similar but larger faults of a worldly manhood. And yet he concludes the first book of his confessions by thanking God for the many mercies and blessings with which he had surrounded his early years.

He spent his sixteenth year at home, and he felt that it was the most decisively fatal year of his moral degeneracy. This was partly due to the fact that it was an idle year. His parents had withdrawn him from a school at Madaura in order to save expense, desiring to send him when he was seventeen to Carthage, 'the Muse of Africa', that he might receive the best education which Africa could furnish.

The withdrawal of school restraints, and the hot blood of an African youth at the most dangerous period of his life, plunged him into impurity, and the shame and misery by which it is accompanied. God was ever present with him in compassionate wrath, sprinkling bitter troubles on forbidden pleasures. He was in the hands of bad companions, and his friendship with them was a vicious friendship which would have been held disgraceful even in human judgements. In that climate and by the customs of that day he was of an age to marry, but his parents, eager for his intellectual progress and worldly advancement, did not seek to restrain his fervid passions within honourable bounds. Patricius, so generous in providing for his studies, was careless of his character. He did not wish his son's prospects to be impeded by a marriage bond. The thorns of lust grew higher than his head in that neglected garden of his soul, and there was no hand to pick them up. His mother saw the danger he was in, and calling him aside, earnestly implored him to live a pure and honourable life. But he had learnt to despise a pure woman's exhortations, instead of accepting them as God's warning to him.

When he heard his companions boasting of their iniquities, he felt quite ashamed of not having gone to quite the same lengths, and wished to do wrong, not only from pleasure in the wrong, but from a desire for the shameful glory of such guilt. 'I became,' he says, 'more vicious that I might not be blamed by them for virtue; and when I had done nothing flagitious enough to match their abandoned conduct, I pretended that I had done what I had not done, that my comparative innocence might not be comparative disgrace, and lest I should be more despised in proportion as I was more chaste.' During this year Augustine recalls with shame an expedition which he made with his comrades to rob a pear-tree. The pears were not good; he did not want them; when he had got them he only flung them to the pigs; he had more and better at home: and yet, after playing with his friends till the dead of night, he joined them in an expedition to strip the tree out of sheer love of what his conscience condemned, and because he liked to join a multitude in doing wrong. A good many schoolboys have robbed orchards, but surely no other schoolboy expresses his remorse in language so heart-breaking as that used by this young African!

After this unfortunate year he went at the age of seventeen to Carthage. It was a splendid city, second in literary distinction to Rome alone; but its streets, of which some were filled with magnificent temples, and others gleamed with gold and marble, did but conceal a deep moral degradation. As in Constantinople and Jerusalem, a nominal Christianity had refined the intellect without reforming the morals. The very Christianity of the place was ferocious, and the drunken revelry which had once disgraced the festivals of demons was now practised over the ashes of martyrs. Here Augustine plunged into the vilest dissipations of great cities, and the theatres which he frequented supplied at once the images of his misery and the fuel to his passions. His words throw a dark and enigmatic shadow over his life, to which we need allude no further than to say that he confesses himself to have been no exception to the universal experience that 'forbidden pleasure is deceitful and envenomed pleasure; its hollowness disappoints at the time; its consequences cruelly torture afterwards; its effects deprave for ever.' 'I was foul,' he says,'and dishonourable, yet in my abounding vanity I strove to be elegant and polished.' Even in the sacred precincts of the church he was guilty of entering into intrigues.

He rose to a high position in the school of the rhetoricians, but he sank at this period to the very nadir of unfaithfulness to God, whose mercy was yet hovering over him, and scourging him during these his offerings to devils. Yet even then he never joined the worst, and what would now be called the most rowdy, class of Carthaginian students. There was a body of them known by the name of 'subverters', whose despicable object it apparently was to introduce disorder and corruption into the classes of all the teachers. The shyness and reticence with which Augustine alludes to these youths makes us fear that they were guilty of worse excesses than mere disorder. Augustine admired their 'deeds of devils' at a distance, and even enjoyed their friendship, but felt an 'impudent shame' that he was not quite as bad and senseless as they were. His father had died soon after he went to Carthage, but the generous friendship of a citizen of Tagaste named Romanianus enabled him to finish his course at the university, and in intellectual respects he does not seem to have wasted his opportunities. To Romanianus he always felt a warm gratitude. 'When I was bereaved of my father, you,' he says, 'consoled me with your friendship, you encouraged me by your exhortations, you assisted me with your wealth.'

In reviewing these confessions we must, as in other cases, beware of being misled into thinking that Augustine was worse than multitudes of other young men of his day. The confessions of the holiest are ever the most bitter in their self-accusation, because saints have learnt to judge their sins not by man's standard, but by Christ's. They read their condemnation not by the pale starlight of human judgement but by the light of the eye of God, which burns into the secrets of their hearts 'ten thousand times brighter than the sun'. In a public address delivered at Carthage many years later as bishop, he confessed that in that city he had most of all lived an evil life, and had been among the number of those whom the Apostle calls 'fools', and to every good work reprobate.

> For although they knew God, they neither glorified him as God nor gave thanks to him, but their thinking became futile and their foolish hearts were darkened. Although they claimed to be wise, they became fools and exchanged the glory of the immortal God for images made to look like mortal man and birds and animals and reptiles. (Romans 1:21–23)

Vincentius, a bishop of the Rogatistae in Carthage, in a letter to him when he was bishop, testifies that even during these godless years the world had regarded him before his conversion as an ardent student of literature, and a man of quiet and honourable demeanour. But the heart knew its own bitterness if other men did not.

A gleam of higher aspiration was introduced into his heart by reading the *Hortensius* of Cicero. The book changed the current of his feelings, and awoke his desire for a better and worthier life. He resumed the habit of prayer, and felt some earnest strivings after God. But the benefit of this loftier influence was to a great extent

counterbalanced by his falling into the heresy of the Manichees, in which he remained for nine years. He turned to
the scriptures 'to see what they were like', but he felt so
complete a contempt for their simplicity, and the absence
from them of the rhetorical graces which he had been
taught to admire above everything, that he very soon
threw them aside. The day was yet far distant when he saw
scripture 'honeyed with heaven's honey and luminous with
its light'. His intellectual vanity had been greatly increased
by his success in all his studies—geometry, music, poetry,
and eloquence—but most of all by the ease with which he
mastered the Categories of Aristotle entirely by himself,
and that so thoroughly that he found nothing to learn
from the oral explanations and diagrams of the best
Carthaginian teachers. His swiftly-moving intellect and
acumen were gifts of God, but he did not sanctify them to
God's service. The Bible was a dead letter to him because
he did not bring to the study of it the requisite humility.
Instead of coming to it as a humble enquirer he came as a
haughty disputant, and so he closed himself against the
door at which he would have been admitted if he had
knocked in humble earnestness.

Hence he fell more easily into the snares of the Manichees. Their 'birdlime' was exactly tempered to win such a
bird as he was. They frequently used the name of Jesus,
and of the Comforter, but to them they were names only.
Their constant cry was 'the Truth! the Truth!' and Augustine, whom the noble eloquence of the *Hortensius* had specially inspired with a love for truth, passionately yearned
to find the goal to which they declared that they alone
could lead him. They professed to live pure and holy lives,
and they appealed at the same time to his natural pride of
intellect. 'The church,' they said, '*imposes* truth upon you
instead of teaching it, and the truth which it offers is composed to a great extent of anile fables, which cannot be
supported by reason. The church demands faith before
reason, and terrifies you into submission by superstitious

threats. We, on the other hand, only invite you to accept truths which we have first explained, and which you can perfectly understand.' Besides this they had at command a multitude of criticisms and objections which charmed the conceit of a proud and garrulous youth fresh from the sophistic victories of the schools. Misinterpretation of scripture furnished them with their strongest weapons. They raised arguments to which he could not reply from the discrepant genealogies of St Matthew and St Luke, which they declared to have been invented by heretics. They sneered and cavilled at large parts of the Old Testament. They had insuperable objections derived from the origin of evil, on which they founded the system of dualism—of a good and an evil deity—a system which has had charms for so many millions of the human race. By such theories and reasonings they appealed to his pride and his intellect, nor did they leave ungratified his tendency to superstition. They had preposterous fancies about fruits, and while they taught Augustine to laugh at the words of prophets and evangelists as old wives' fables, they persuaded him to believe such pernicious nonsense as that vegetables have sentient life; 'that a plucked fig weeps milky tears for the loss of its mother tree, and yet, that if a saint eats it after it has been plucked by the crime of another, he would receive angels—yea, even particles of the Divine—into his own system, and breathe them forth, whereas these particles of the true God would have been bound in the fruit if they were not loosed by the teeth and stomach of an elect saint'! But worse than all else, Augustine derived from their teaching a spirit of self-excuse for his own sins. They seemed less heinous when he was led to regard them as due not so much to his own will as to the external tyranny of some evil power.

At first Augustine was so thoroughly entangled in the nets of this heresy that, 'with a most wretched and most mad loquacity', he devastated the Catholic faith, and caught some of his best friends in the snare of logomachy in which he had himself been entangled. His friend and pupil Alypius, his kind patron Romanianus, and Honoratus, who was not yet a Christian, were brought over by him into Manicheism.

For nine years Augustine continued to be a Manichean, and the system exercised a deep influence over his mind, even after he had abandoned it. Yet it never satisfied him. He found no real rest in it. He soon discovered that the Manicheans were far more successful in destructive than in constructive arguments. He found that they had little to offer him except such captious and profane questions as whether he supposed that God was corporeal, and had hands and nails, or whether persons who committed murders were to be regarded as saints. As long as they confined themselves to disparagement of the Old Testament, or to questions that bore upon insoluble mysteries, they seemed formidable; but they had little else to offer. The soul cannot live upon negations, or upon the monstrous hypothesis of two Gods, one good, one evil. He would never become one of their 'presbyters', or their 'elect'; he was only a 'hearer', and, as such, did not receive their baptism or attend their Eucharist, about which he could get no information. Between his nineteenth and twenty-ninth years he was bidden to await the arrival at Carthage of their great bishop and champion Faustus; and during that period he held to the Manicheans mainly because an imperfect apprehension of the nature of scripture and of the Catholic faith had left him unable to cope with their objections.

Another fatal influence during these years was of a moral character. When he was seventeen he formed an illicit union with a woman, with whom indeed he lived faithfully, but to whom he was never wedded. The following year she bore him a son, to whom he gave the name of Adeodatus, of whose precocious genius and early death we shall speak later on.

It is strange to our notions, and it shows the evil

tendency to place orthodoxy above holiness, that while Monnica was unspeakably distressed by Augustine's heresy, we do not read that she uttered a single word of remonstrance about his living for so many years with a woman who was not his wife. When her son became a Manichee, she indignantly excluded him altogether from her house and table, but she afterwards readmitted him to live under her roof, in spite of the immoral bond by which he was defamed. Much, of course, must be allowed for the differing moral standards of different ages and countries. The testimony of many authorities shows us that at this period the practice had become common even among the clergy, whose marriage was discouraged by an ignorant public opinion. But the conscience of Augustine, though less tender on this subject than we might have expected, was not wholly seared. He fully recognised that he was living a life of sin.

Monnica wept over the young Manichee as sorely as though he were dead, and she offered to God her constant prayers for his conversion to the true faith. That conversion was long delayed, but she was not left without consolation. She had a dream which greatly comforted her. She dreamt that she was standing on a wooden plank overwhelmed with grief and sorrow, when she saw a youth approach her, resplendent, joyous, and with a smile upon his face. He asked her the reason for her sadness and her daily tears, and she answered that she was bewailing the perdition of her son. He bade her banish her anxiety, and to observe that where she was, there her son was too. Turning to Augustine in her dream, she saw him standing near her on the same wooden plank. 'Whence came this,' he asks, 'except because thy ears, O thou merciful omnipotent, were at her heart, O thou who carest for each one of us as though caring for him alone, and carest for all as much as for each of us?' When Monnica related to him the dream, Augustine said it only showed that she would come over to his opinions. 'Not so,' she answered with quick intelligence, 'the angel did not say to me "where *he* is there you will be," but "where *you* are there he will be".'

In her deep desire to win him from his errors, Monnica often entreated others to plead with him, and, among them, a faithful bishop who had been trained in the scriptures. The bishop, however, with wise insight, declined to do so. He saw that nothing could be gained from a conflict with

> the rattling tongue
> Of saucy and audacious eloquence,

in which the youth's pride might only be further inflamed by the semblance of a dialectic victory. 'Leave him there,' he said, 'and only pray God for him; he will discover by reading what is his error, and how great his impiety. I was myself once a Manichee. I not only read nearly all their books, but even copied them out, and without any controversy I discovered how much that sect should be avoided.' But Monnica still continued to entreat his assistance with floods of tears. Then, with a touch of impatience, he replied in memorable words, which she accepted as a voice from heaven: 'Go,' he said, 'live so; it cannot be that the son of those tears will perish.'

2

Manichee

When Augustine's education at Carthage was finished he returned to Tagaste, where he lived by giving literary instruction, which was called 'teaching grammar'. His kind and generous patron Romanianus received him into his house, and they lived in such close intimacy that Augustine almost seemed to be a partner himself at this period of his life to the Prodigal Son, shut out from the husks of the swine which he was feeding. Among his hearers was the excellent Alypius, a kinsman of Romanianus, son of one of the principal burghers of Tagaste, who afterwards became the Bishop of Tagaste, and was one of his lifelong friends.

At Tagaste he had another friend, whose name is left unmentioned, but to whom he was bound by the closest attachment. They had been boys together, had gone to school together, had played together, had studied together as youths, and were completely one in heart and mind, lacking only the bond of mutual piety, which is indispensable for a pure and perfect friendship. Augustine had dragged this friend with him from the true faith into the pernicious falsities of Mancheism. The young man fell dangerously ill, and while he lay in a deep torpor he was baptised without his previous consent. Augustine did not oppose the baptism, because he felt sure that if his friend recovered he would hold fast to the principles of Manicheism.

He did recover, and Augustine, who was constantly at his bedside, took the earliest opportunity to laugh at his baptism. But he, with a sudden outburst of independence, rebuked Augustine, and said that if he spoke in that manner again their friendship must cease. A few days later he had a relapse, and died. So bitter and overwhelming was the grief of Augustine that he seemed to see death everywhere. He wept abundantly, but he could not pray. Life at Tagaste became insupportable to him, and his anguish was the more poignant because it was so extremely self-observant. He could not get rid of the fatal luxury of his woe. In order to escape from a place where every sight and sound reminded him of what he had lost, he threw up his employment and returned to Carthage. His heart was peculiarly formed for friendship. Nothing on earth seemed to him so sweet as to talk and laugh together with his friends; to exchange benefits; to read eloquent books; to be serious or to trifle; to differ occasionally without animosity, and to find all the greater delight in constant agreement; to teach and to learn in turns; to long for the absent with regret, to welcome their visits with joy, to gaze on their faces, to grasp their hands, to hear their words.

At Carthage he exchanged the drudgery of a grammarian for the more distinguished post of a teacher of rhetoric, and until he was able to make his own way Romanianus supplied his needs. 'I taught,' he says, 'in those years the art of rhetoric and victorious loquacity for gain. Yet my chief desire was to have good pupils, to whom without wiliness I taught wiles, not that they might injure the innocent, but might sometimes defend the guilty.' His desire for good pupils was not quite in vain, for he numbered among them two promising sons of Romanianus, as well as Eulogius, who afterwards became a distinguished teacher at Carthage, and Alypius, whom he regarded as both good and learned. The father of Alypius had quarrelled with Augustine, and for some time the youth did not like to attend his lectures. Augustine heard with sorrow that he had become passionately fond of the games of the circus, but, from the relations between them, and because he thought that the youth sided with his father, he was unable to warn him either as a tutor or as a friend.

Soon, however, Alypius began to come and hear his lectures again, going away directly he had finished. One day Augustine was sitting with his pupils round him in the open air when Alypius joined them. Augustine happened to be explaining some book which led him quite accidentally to allude to the Circensian games, and he spoke of them with derisive sarcasm, without even thinking of the presence of Alypius. Alypius might have been offended, but instead of that he showed the truth of the proverb of Solomon, 'Rebuke a wise man and he will love you' (Proverbs 9:8). From that day forward he abandoned the games, felt a deeper love for Augustine, who had delivered him from such a temptation, and persuaded his father to let him become his pupil once more. Won by the ostentation of continence which prevailed among the Manichees, Alypius also joined Augustine in his heretical communion.

The prize of a crown was annually given at Carthage for the best poem, and for this prize Augustine determined to compete. When this became known a pagan augur came to him and asked him what he would give to win the crown by his magic arts. Augustine rejected the offered magic with indignation, and told the augur that if the crown were even golden and immortal, he would not have so much as a fly killed on his behalf; for he believed that the augur wished to invoke the demons in his favour by animal sacrifices. He won the prize, however, and the crown was placed on his head by the proconsul Vindicianus.

There was at Carthage a diviner named Albicerius, who, though he was a man of disgraceful character, was consulted even by persons of eminence. One day a pupil of Augustine's challenged Albicerius to tell him of what he was thinking. 'A verse of Virgil,' was the reply. It was actually the case, and he then asked, 'What verse?' Albicerius was a man of no education, yet he at once repeated the verse. On another occasion a gentleman of proconsular rank named Flaccianus was thinking of buying a farm, and asked Albicerius whether he could advise him about a matter which he had on hand. Albicerius at once replied, 'You are thinking of buying the farm at ——,' mentioning the name of the place, though it was so out of the way that even Flaccianus could scarcely remember it. We who are accustomed to thought-reading and conjuring tricks should hardly place Albicerius as high as Cagliostro or Houdini; but Flaccianus and Augustine attributed his responses to some abject demon, and advised everyone to keep aloof from him.

Augustine for many years believed in astrology and studied horoscopes; and all the more because it was comforting to a guilty conscience to lay the blame for his misdoings on the constellation under which he was born. He believed that the answers of the astrologers were often correct, although he could find no clear explanation for the fact. In vain his friend Nebridius, a youth of great capacity, ridiculed the whole science. In vain Vindicianus, who was a distinguished physician, advised him to leave such studies alone and to earn his livelihood solely by rhetoric, telling him that he had himself thoroughly studied astrology, and had once meant to earn his bread by it, but had found it to be a baseless imposture.

Augustine never quite abandoned his belief in it, till once when he was consulted by a dear friend of much distinction named Firminus, who asked him to find out if the constellations favoured some ambitious hope which he then entertained. Augustine replied that he would do so, though he was now more than half persuaded that there was nothing to be learned from such enquiries. Firminus, though he retained a belief which he had learnt from his father, told a story about himself which finally convinced Augustine to abandon astrology. He said that at the very instant of his own birth a slave of his mother's had also brought forth a son. The horoscope of the two infants must, therefore, have been entirely identical, and yet Firminus had grown up in wealth, rank, and honour, while the sharer in his natal moment continued to be at that moment a poor and humble slave. This story, and the reflection that Esau and Jacob, who were so widely different in their destinies, must have had exactly the same horoscopes, completed the deliverance of Augustine from an empty superstition. Henceforth he attributed correct predictions of astrology to the same accident which often gives significance to the Sortes Biblicae and the Sortes Virgilianae.

Augustine always retained a certain amount of cautious belief in the intimations of dreams. In one of his later letters, in answer to a question of Evodius about the soul, he tells a story of a 'beloved physician' at Carthage named Gennadius, who, though a good man and earnest in his beneficence to the poor, had doubts about the future life. His doubts were entirely removed by two dreams. One night he dreamt that a noble-looking youth came to him and said, 'Follow me.' He followed, and was led to a city in which he heard strains of delicious music and hymns and psalms, and the youth told him that this was the singing of the blessed. Awaking, he found it was a dream, and attached no importance to it. But on another night the same youth came again and asked, 'Do you remember me?' 'Yes,' answered Gennadius. 'I saw you in my dream, and you took me to hear the songs of the blessed.' 'Are you dreaming now?' 'Yes.' 'Where is your body at this moment?' 'In my bed.' 'Your eyes, then, are closed and bound in sleep?' 'Yes.' 'How is it, then, that you see me?' Gennadius could give no answer, and the angel said, 'Just as you see me without the eyes of the flesh, so it will be when all your senses are removed by death. Take care that henceforth you have no doubts about the life to come.' You may say that this was a dream, adds Augustine, and anyone may think what he likes about it. Nevertheless there are, he implies, some dreams which have a divine significance.

This dream of Gennadius is narrated in reply to a letter of Evodius in which he had mentioned the story of a young notary of Uzalis, of which town Evodius was bishop. The boy was the son of a presbyter, and showed such skill, diligence, and promise, that the bishop employed him as his reader and secretary. He had desired to die early, and as he lay dying he sang. He signed himself with the cross, and died a virginal youth. Two days after, a widow named Urbica saw in a dream a deacon, who had died four years before, preparing a palace of silver which he said was to be the dead youth's home, and then an old man dressed in white ordered two angels in white robes to lift the youth's body to heaven; after which roses, known by the name of virgin roses, began to blossom on his tomb. The youth himself had seen before his death the vision of a young friend who said that he had come to fetch him; and his father the presbyter was warned of his own approaching death by visions of the dead youth both to himself and to a brother-monk. Augustine is very much pleased with the story, but professes his inability to offer any adequate explanation.

At the age of twenty-six or twenty-seven Augustine wrote his first book. It was *On the Fitting and the Beautiful*, and is no longer extant. He dedicated it to a Roman orator named Hierius, who was personally unknown to him, but whose works and sayings he admired.

When he was twenty-nine he began to be greatly shaken in his Manichean opinions. A certain suspicion about the practices of the elders had prevented him from ever assuming any rank beyond that of 'hearer', which was the lowest in their order. He had indeed seen nothing of those impure mysteries with which Epiphanius charged them, and which they perhaps regarded, at least in some of their sects, as necessary concessions to the evil power. But during nine years it had been his unvarying experience that every one of their 'elect' who was personally known to him had either been detected in vice, or had given grounds for grave suspicion.

On one occasion he had seen more than three of the elect, who lived in different houses, walking together in the streets of Carthage after one of their meetings; and they behaved in a manner so shamefully immoral that Augustine and others who witnessed their misconduct saw that they exercised no restraint upon each other's conduct. A complaint was made, but they were left entirely unpunished, evidently from a dread of what they might reveal. On another occasion, when a vigil was being observed, the lights were suddenly put out, and a number of the elect were charged with conduct which even pagans would have condemned as disgraceful.

These, and many other flagitious circumstances, which he relates in his book *On the Character of the Manicheans*, entirely shook his faith in their professions of temperance, soberness, and chastity. He saw their leaders to be envious, avaricious, quarrelsome, slanderous, and addicted to the dangerous vices of city life.

He was further confirmed in his belief that the Manichees were insincere by the total failure of a fervent and wealthy 'hearer' named Constantius to establish at Rome a sort of monastery in which the best of the elect should be maintained at his expense, and should live, really as well as professedly, under the rule of Manes. At first none of the Manichean bishops would support him, but at length he explained his plan to a rustic bishop who was willing to join him. A community of the elect was then formed, but a very short experience was sufficient to stamp it with hopeless failure. The elect soon began to quarrel vehemently among themselves, and to denounce each other for the worst crimes; and at last they came in a body and declared that the new rules were absolutely intolerable. 'They must either be capable of being kept,' answered Constantius, 'or our founder must have been an utter fool.' The community broke up; the bishop fled. After his flight it was found that he had a bag full of money, and that from this secret store he had supplied himself with food in habitual defiance of the rule. Constantius then headed the Manichean schism of the Mattarii, so called because they slept on mats; but shortly after he embraced the Catholic faith and was still living when Augustine wrote his books against Faustus.

Augustine was further shaken in his heresy by intellectual doubts. There came to Carthage a lecturer named Helpidius who advanced scriptural arguments to which the Manichees were only able to whisper among their hearers the baseless answer that the New Testament had been largely interpolated—an assertion in favour of which they could not adduce a single manuscript.

He felt, too, that they did not, after all, solve the tremendous difficulty about the origin of evil. If the soul was a particle of God, why should he have placed it in mortal bodies which belonged to the devil? Nebridius had an argument which seemed to him decisive. He asked the Manichees what the powers of evil would have done to God if he had not struggled against them. If they could have done him harm, then God must be violable and corruptible; if he was beyond their power, why should he have mingled with their matter a portion of himself? In fact, Augustine was beginning to doubt whether matter was essentially evil, and the puerile answer, that 'if a man held a scorpion in his hand he would find it evil enough', only disgusted him. He began to think that the philosophers, especially the Academics, were far abler than the Manichees, and that their science at any rate was far more rational and correct. He was bidden, however, to await the coming of Faustus, who would triumphantly vindicate the doctrine of Manes and make everything clear.

Augustine was twenty-nine when Faustus at last arrived. He was an African of the town of Milevis. His birth was obscure, but his ability had raised him to the position of the chief bishop of the Manichees. He boasted that he had abandoned all things—even father and mother and wife and children—for the gospel's sake; that he had neither silver nor gold nor brass in his purse; that he had no care for the morrow, what he should eat or what he should be clothed with, and that he had fulfilled and experienced all the beatitudes for the truth's sake. In spite of which he slept on downy couches, was softly clad, and lived with a luxury which not only displeased the Mattarii, but was far beyond the condition of his birth. The only persecution he braved was a short and easy deportation with some of his followers to a certain island. He knew something of 'grammar', but in all the other sciences his attainments were exceedingly moderate. Besides the Manichean writings he had only read some orations of Cicero, a very few books of Seneca, and some of the poets.

He was, however, a graceful and fluent speaker, and habitual practice enabled him to trick out commonplaces in a sort of silvery and attractive eloquence, which was rendered more effective by his apparent modesty and sincerity. He had written a book against the God of the Old Testament and the Incarnation, which, when it fell into Augustine's hands, he was able to refute word for word. To many Faustus was a 'snare of death', but without his knowledge and against his will he finally emancipated Augustine from the net of heresy.

For Augustine saw through him. Personally he liked him, and he was pleased with the modest readiness with which Faustus expressed his entire inability to help Augustine in any of the pseudo-scientific Manichean questions, or any of his more recondite spiritual difficulties. He conversed and read with Faustus, but finding that this boasted champion had so little to say in defence of essential doctrines, he gave up all intention of penetrating any deeper into the mysteries of the sect.

3

Rome

A great change was now at hand. Augustine was entirely weary of Carthage, and made up his mind to go to Rome. He was not wholly insensible to the arguments of his friends that there he would win greater fame and a larger income, but his chief inducement was the humiliation caused him by the turbulent folly of the 'upsetters', those young hoodlums of Carthage. These silly youths, protected by a bad custom, were allowed to burst into the classes of any professor whom they chose to disturb, and there to break up the lecture and ruin all discipline. He was ashamed to think that he had associated with these noisy gangs in his own student days, though he had not approved of their proceedings; but now that he was a teacher they rendered his life miserable. His enemies afterwards charged him with having been driven from Africa by the decree of the proconsul Messianus against the Manichees, a calumny which he was easily able to refute because that decree was not promulgated till a year later.

Knowing that he should encounter considerable opposition, and especially from his mother, he kept secret his purpose of sailing to Italy. Romanianus, who had helped him with such ungrudging kindness, and whose son Augustine was leaving at Carthage, was indignant that he had not been consulted; but Augustine succeeded in explaining to him his reasons, and the two continued to be warm friends.

Monnica discovered his intention, and when he started out she determined to leave Tagaste with him, either to bring him home with her or at all costs to accompany him. In vain he tried to deceive her by saying that he was only going to see the last of a friend who was about to sail. She declined to return home, and at last he only escaped by a descreditable ruse. He persuaded her to land and pass the night in a chapel consecrated to the memory of the martyr Cyprian. There she spent the hours of darkness in tears and in prayer to God that he would prevent the voyage of her son. Augustine meanwhile had secretly withdrawn himself, and spread his sails for Rome with a favouring wind. She filled the shore with her lamentations, upbraiding him for his cruelty and fraud. When her mind was calmer she returned home and never ceased to pray for him; and the time came when she and her son alike recognised in all these events the invisible guidance of the hand of love.

At Rome he was the guest of a Manichean who, like himself, was a 'hearer', and he was thrown almost exclusively into the society of the Manichees and their 'elect'. Although he warned his host against the acceptance of all their fables, he still clung to their pestilent doctrine that sin was an involuntary action, and therefore needed no repentance. He was hindered, too, by the falsehood, which the heretics had instilled into him, that the Catholic Church believed God to be corporeal, a doctrine which he despised. But he became more and more inclined to adopt the views of the Academics, that assent about most things should be held in suspense, and that truth is in reality undiscoverable.

His stay at Rome was short. He arrived in 383, and soon found that the profession of a teacher in the capital of the empire was attended with disadvantages still more serious than those which had driven him from the capital of Africa. He was free indeed from the boisterous incursions of the 'upsetters', which were forbidden by the Roman law; but on the other hand the Roman students had a disgraceful way of cheating the professors of their fees. When they had learnt as much as they could, they conspired together and passed in a body to another lecture-room, without discharging their debt to the first teacher, so that Augustine found himself in a worse case than before. This position was rendered all the more trying by the vapid nature of the instruction which he proposed to give.

From this serious difficulty he was liberated by his most opportune election to a professorship at Milan. The nomination to this post had been placed in the hands of the distinguished pagan statesman and man of letters, Symmachus, who, after hearing Augustine deliver a public declamation, placed the office at his disposal. He had appealed to his Manichean friends to interest themselves in his favour, and they little suspected that one of his motives in desiring to go to Milan was to be rid of them. His success seemed to open to him a new career. He was to be transported to Milan without expense in the public vehicles, and was to have a fixed salary in addition to his fees.

To Milan, accordingly, he went in 385, and there he was speedily joined by his friend Alypius, whose experiences at Rome had been very trying. He had gone thither at the wish of his parents to study the law, and had determined never to be present at one of the cruel and hated gladiatorial spectacles. One day, however, he met some friends who were returning from a dinner, and they with familiar violence declared that they would take him to the amphitheatre, where the deadly games were then being exhibited.

'You may drag my body there,' he said, when he had tried in vain to resist them, 'but you cannot drag either my eyes or my mind to these horrors. So I shall be at once present and absent, and shall conquer both you and them.'

In spite of this they took him with them, to see whether his firmness would hold out. On entering, they secured places, and found the vast multitude passionately absorbed in the fierce delight. Alypius closed his eyes, and forbade his mind to share in such crimes; but alas, he did not also close his ears! At some thrilling crisis of the combat he was startled by the mighty shout of the spectators, and while still determined to hate and despise whatever he should see, he was driven by curiosity to open his eyes. Instantly, says Augustine, his soul received a deadlier wound than that of the poor gladiator who was being

> Butchered to make a Roman holiday.

Lord Houghton describes the scene in his 'Fall of Alypius':

> The love of contest and the lust of blood
> Dwell in the depths of man's original heart,
> And at mere shows and names of wise and good
> Will not from their barbaric homes depart,
> But half-asleep await their time, and then
> Bound forth like tigers from their jungle-den.
>
> And all the curious wickerwork of thought,
> Of logical result and learned skill,
> Of precepts with examples interwrought,
> Of high ideals and determinate will,
> The careful fabric of ten thousand hours
> Is crushed beneath the moment's brutal powers.
>
> . . . . .
>
> The rage subsided; the deep sandy floor
> Sucked the hot blood; the hook like some vile prey
> Dragged off the noble body of the Moor.
> The victor, doomed to die some other day,
> Enjoyed the plaudits purposelessly earned—
> And back Alypius to himself returned.

For when he saw the rush of crimson over the victim's armour he was swept away by the wild excitement. He

became, as it were, drunk with the savage passion for
blood.

No longer averting his eyes, he gazed heart and soul on
the brutal scene before him, indifferent to the guilt and
intoxicated with the remorseless pleasure of the contest.
He was no longer the Alypius who had entered the
amphitheatre, but one of the crowd to which he had joined
himself, and a true companion of those whom he had
resisted. It is needless to say more. He gazed, he shouted,
his soul took fire. He went away with a frenzy which stimu-
lated him to return not only *with* those who had forced him
there, but even *before* them, and he took others with him.
Nor was it till long afterwards that God rescued him from
this new peril.

The following fine passage from a recent poet will illustrate the fierce passion for the games which swayed so
many Roman hearts:

Marcus, abiding in Jerusalem,
Greeting to Caius, his best friend in Rome!
Salve! these presents will be borne to you
By Lucius, who is wearied with this place,
Sated with travel, looks upon the East
As simply hateful—blazing, barren, bleak—
And longs again to find himself in Rome.
After the tumult of its streets, its trains
Of slaves and clients, and its villas cool
With marble porticoes beside the sea,
And friends and banquets,—more than all, its games,—
This life seems blank and flat. He pants to stand
In its vast circus all alive with heads
And quivering arms and floating robes,—the air
Thrilled by the roaring *fremitus* of men,—
The sunlit awning heaving overhead,
Swollen and strained against its corded veins,
And flapping out its hem with loud report,—
The wild beasts roaring from the pit below,—

The wilder crowd responding from above
With one long yell that sends the startled blood
With thrill and sudden flush into the cheeks,—
A hundred trumpets screaming,—the dull thump
Of horses galloping across the sand,—
The clang of scabbards, the sharp clash of steel,—
Live swords, that whirl a circle of gray fire,—
Brass helmets flashing 'neath their streaming hair,—
A universal tumult—all eyes straining down
To the arena's pit—all lips set close—
All muscles strained,—and then that sudden yell,
Habet!—That's Rome, says Lucius: so it is!
That is, 'tis *his* Rome,—'tis not yours and mine.

Alypius had another very disagreeable adventure. Augustine had taught him the custom of walking about while he prepared a speech, and for this purpose he had gone at noonday into the forum. He was pacing by himself in front of the tribunal with his tablets and stylus, when another student entered unnoticed with an axe in his hand. His object was to steal the lead from the fencing which projected over the street of the silversmiths. These artisans heard the blows of the axe and sent for the *aeditimi*, who acted as police of the forum, to arrest the depredator. He heard them coming, dropped his axe, and fled. Alypius noticed his hasty exit, and curious as to the reason of his flight, went to the spot. Seeing the axe there, he picked it up and looked at it. At that moment the officers came in and seized him.

The circumstantial evidence against him looked very strong. The blows of an axe had been heard, and he had been caught alone on the spot with an axe in his hand. Regarding him as a thief who had been detected in the act, the scum of the quorum gathered round him, and he was taken off to the judge. His imprisonment and punishment seemed certain, and everything was going against him, when fortunately the captors and crowd were met by an architect who had special charge of the public buildings. They were delighted to show him the ostensible culprit in the thefts of which they had themselves been frequently suspected. The architect had met Alypius in the house of a senator, and recognising him took him by the hand. Leading him aside, he learnt the true facts of the case. He ordered the turbulent crowd to follow him, and they went to the house of the youth who really had been guilty. Before the door of the house they found a little slave-boy whom Alypius had seen following the student as a page. The boy was too young to be on his guard, and when they showed him the axe and asked whose it was, he at once answered, 'It is ours,' and on being cross-examined told the whole story. Thus the friend of Augustine was saved from the degradation of being condemned as a common thief.

In spite of these adventures Alypius had risen to great distinction. He was appointed an assessor to the Count of the Italian Treasury, and had proved both that he was incorruptible and that he was courageous. A very powerful senator, who was much feared by many, endeavoured to procure for himself an illegal privilege. Alypius boldly resisted the claim and contemptuously spurned the bribe which was offered him, although even the Count of the Treasury had not ventured openly to refuse the senator's request, and had indeed purposely devolved the responsibility upon his youthful and courageous deputy. Alypius was indeed nearly tempted by the privilege of having books copied for him at Praetorian prices, 'but consulting justice he altered his determination for the better, esteeming equity whereby he was hindered more gainful than the power whereby he was allowed. These are slight things,' says Augustine, 'but he that is faithful in little is faithful also in much.'

4

Conversion

Arrived at Milan, Augustine took the earliest opportunity to go and hear the great Bishop Ambrose. 'I was led to him unknowingly by God,' he says, 'that I might knowingly be led to God by him.' Ambrose received him with fatherly kindness, and Augustine felt himself powerfully attracted by his commanding personality. He loved him at first, not as a teacher of truth, but as one who was kind towards himself. He stood in the crowded basilica and listened with pleasure to his sermons, but merely because they were eloquent and attractive. He found them less polished and silvery than those of Faustus, but incomparably superior in thought and matter. Almost without his knowing it, the meaning of what Ambrose said, as well as his language, became to him a matter of interest.

Two things he learnt which were to him of inestimable value. The Manichees had always assured him that the Catholics believed in a corporeal God, and that this was their interpretation of the verse, 'in the image of God he created him' (Genesis 1:27). This he found to be an ignorant misinterpretation, and the discovery brought a deep sense of relief to his mind. Then he also understood for the first time how to overcome the difficulties which Ambrose had learnt from the teaching of Origen. Augustine realised that the key to interpreting scripture was the method of allegorising, and the text, 'the letter kills, but the Spirit gives life' (2 Corinthians 3:6), was constantly on his lips. The key was not the right one, and the text was entirely misapplied from its original sense; but it took the world a thousand years more to learn the true principles of exegesis, and meanwhile a very partial truth was the providential means by which Augustine was delivered from decided errors.

His deliverance was hastened by the arrival of Monnica, who, with devoted affection, took Navigius, her younger son, and followed her elder son to Milan. Monnica almost lived in the Ambrosian basilica, and nothing could exceed her joy when Augustine informed her that, though not a Catholic, he had at any rate ceased to be a Manichee, and had offered himself as a catechumen in the church of his mother. Ambrose formed a high opinion of Monnica, and spoke of her to Augustine with warm praise. Augustine continued to be a constant hearer of his sermons, and longed for some opportunity to lay before him all his doubts and hesitations. Ambrose was perfectly accessible. The door of his house was open, and anyone who wished might come to see him unannounced. But he was besieged by such a crowd of visitors, and so constantly occupied in business, that Augustine never found an opportunity for a lengthened conversation, for, when the business of the day was finished, he always found Ambrose reading so diligently and so devoutly that he did not like to disturb him.

The only question which he had the chance of asking was one in which he felt no interest, and only asked at his mother's request. To Monnica, the wish of Ambrose was law. In Africa she had been accustomed to offer vegetables and bread and wine at the feasts of the martyrs, and when she came to the door of the church in Milan to do the same, she was informed that Ambrose disapproved of the custom, partly because it too closely resembled the custom of the heathen, and partly because it fostered the temptation to drunkenness. She at once abandoned the custom, and gave to the poor instead.

It had been a custom in the African church to fast on Saturday, and Monnica found an opposite custom prevalent at Milan. When Augustine questioned Ambrose on the subject, he wisely replied that in such a matter it was best to follow the practices of the church to which a person belonged at the time. This comparatively trivial matter was the only one on which he was able to get the private advice of the great bishop.

He was far from happy. Most of his time was occupied with pupils. He had no leisure to read as Ambrose did, and he had no money to buy books, and he was sinking into a settled despair as to the possibility of finding truth, or of ordering his divided life in a way to give him any satisfaction.

His friends shared his perplexities. Nebridius had abandoned home and all things else for the sake of living with him, but he had not yet offered himself for baptism. Alypius, in resisting alike the bribes and the threats which had assailed his legal office, had shown the innocence and integrity of his soul. But there was a magnetism in the character of Augustine which prevented his friends from advancing farther than himself. What he was, they were; and though it was now nearly twelve years since his ardour had been kindled by reading the *Hortensius*, he seemed to himself to have made no real progress.

At one time the little band of friends had seriously discussed a plan for founding a sort of philosophic community in which they could live a coenobitic life, and devote themselves to contemplation far from the troubles of the world. Romanianus, who had been brought to Milan by a lawsuit, and whose wealth rendered the plan feasible, entirely approved of it. But a fatal objection arose. Some of them were married, others intended to marry. What was to be done with their wives?

Augustine himself thought it best to marry, and his mother urged him to do so. He admired Ambrose, and thought that the career of such a man, whose piety had won him such a great place in the empire, was extremely to be envied; but he would not purchase even this at the price of celibacy. The infatuation to which he had been brought by a course which his own conscience had always condemned affected even Alypius, who would have been entirely content to live unmarried had it not been that Augustine declared it to be impossible for himself.

Accordingly, they looked out for and found a young girl who had a little money of her own, and to whom Augustine was to be married in two years, as she was not yet old enough for wedlock. We pass over with shame one of the worst acts of his life. It was a condition of the marriage that he should send away the woman with whom he had lived so long, and to whom he was deeply attached. He sent her away from her son Adeodatus, and from himself, with whom she had lived faithfully though not in marriage. She vowed that she would return to Africa, and live thenceforward a life of perfect purity. He dismissed her, and never mentions her again. It is impossible not to have compassion on this wronged, patient, helpless, forgotten victim; impossible to suppress a movement of indignation against the cold selfishness with which Augustine treated her, as

Into the dark she glides, a silent shame
And a veiled memory, without a name.
And the world knoweth not what words she prayed,
    With what her wail before the altar wept,
What tale she told, what penitence she made,
    What measure by her beating heart was kept.
Nor in what vale or mountain the earth lies
Upon the passionate Carthaginian's eyes.

Well that one penitent hath found such grace
    As to be silent in the silent years,
That no light hand hath lifted from her face
    The silver veil, enwoven by her tears;
Well that one book at least, at least one sod,
Keeps close one tender secret of our God.

And yet he was so deeply entangled in the effeminacy of guilty self-indulgence that he formed another illicit union until his future bride should be old enough to marry. Monnica, little understanding the nature of sin, and sharing the mechanical view of the sacraments which was already universal, thought that when he was once safely married he could be baptised, and that baptism would wash away all previous transgressions. Even in his present strange condition he often entreated his mother to ask God to give her, by a dream, some indication about the future marriage; but she only saw vain and fantastic images which she could not mistake for divine guidance.

But every successive incident of his life was now hastening him to the conversion which was only delayed by his sinful passions. On one occasion he was intensely anxious about a public panegyric which he was to pronounce upon the young emperor Valentinian before a crowded assembly. While his mind was full of the lies which he meant to utter, and which the multitude of his admiring auditors *knew* to be lies, he saw in a street of Milan a drunken beggar, and, in the foul and transient hilarity of this poor wretch, he saw an image of his own worldly desires. He felt inclined to adopt the view of Epicurus, that happiness was the sole end of life; and was only prevented from doing so by that fear of future retribution which he had never been able to shake off. He gradually acquired a truer knowledge of God, and, from Platonic books which the orator Victorinus had translated into Latin, he gained some conception of the eternal Logos, though not as yet of the incarnate Word. The study of St Paul increased his knowledge, and abated his pride.

Every good impression which he had received was deepened by a visit to the presbyter Simplicianus, the spiritual father of Ambrose and his ultimate successor. Simplicianus had been well acquainted with Victorinus, and when Augustine mentioned that he had been reading his translation from Plato, Simplicianus gave him the story of the great orator's conversion. He had been a heathen, and numbered among his pupils some of the noblest senators of Rome, who, in their gratitude, had erected him a statue in the forum. A diligent though secret study of the scriptures had changed his views, and, coming to Simplicianus, he had said to him, 'You may now know that I am a Christian.'

'I will believe it,' said Simplicianus, 'when I see you in church.'

'What?' said Victorinus. 'Do *walls* make Christians?'

The same remark was always met by the same reply, for Victorinus did not dare to offend his crowds of friends and admirers. At last, however, he feared that if he denied Christ on earth Christ would deny him in heaven, and said to Simplicianus, 'Let us go to the church; I wish to become a Christian.'

Shortly afterwards he received public baptism, to the astonishment of Rome and the joy of the church. When he entered the church there was a loud murmur of 'Victorinus! Victorinus!' then a deep silence as he rose to pronounce the confession of faith; and then they carried him home with shouts of congratulation. When Julian passed his edict forbidding Christians to teach heathen literature, Victorinus had crowned his self-sacrifice by closing his school. Augustine longed to make a similar offering to God, but he was enchained by his besetting sin. Perverse will had brought forth lust; lust yielded to had become habit; habit unresisted had developed into the linked fetters of a fatal and slavish though imaginary necessity.

He was yet more deeply moved by a conversation with Pontitianus, a fellow-countryman, who held high military rank in the palace. He was alone with Alypius, whose assessorship had ended, when Pontitianus came to see them. A table for playing some game was before them, and on it lay a book. When Pontitianus took it up he found to his surprise that it contained the epistles of St Paul. He was a Christian, and smiling at Augustine, he congratulated him on such studies. They began to talk on Christian subjects, and among other things Pontitianus told them the story of the hermit St Antony, of whom they had never even heard. The ardent souls of the young men were intensely interested by all that their friend had to tell them about the sainted eremite, and he proceeded to talk to them about monasteries and the lives of monks, of which they had heard nothing, not even being aware that Ambrose was the patron of a monastery just outside the walls of Milan. He then told them that once at Trèves he and three of his brother officers had gone to walk in some gardens near the walls, and that two of them, separating from the rest, had entered a cottage of poor monks in which they found a *Life of Antony*. They were so deeply impressed by it that one of them asked his comrade why they should not at once abandon the path of ambition and become friends and servants of God. Together they made the vow that they would do so, and when Pontitianus came to tell them that it was now dark and they must return, they told him the marvellous change which had now decided their future course. Pontitianus and his friend wept, yet congratulated them, and entreating them for their prayers, returned to the palace. Both of them were betrothed, but they left their future brides, who, fired with the same enthusiasm, took on themselves the vow of perpetual virginity.

The effect of this narrative upon the mind of Augustine was overwhelming. He felt himself a new man. In earlier days he had prayed to God to make him pure, with the secret wish that his prayer might not yet be heard. Now he poured forth that prayer with all his heart. In a tumult of agitation he exclaimed to Alypius, 'What is our state? What have you heard? What is this? The unlearned rise and take heaven by force, and we, with our learning but without heart, see we are rolling ourselves in flesh and blood! Do we blush to follow because they have gone before, and do we not blush not at least to follow?'

Alypius looked at him with astonishment. His emotion

was beyond all wont; his forehead, cheeks, eyes, colour, and tones of voice were more eloquent than his words. Their house had a little garden attached to it, and Augustine rushed into it, followed by Alypius. They sat down as far from the house as possible, and there Augustine, with Alypius sitting silently beside him, fought out the battle with his own tumultuous soul. But even the presence of Alypius, who shared all his secrets, became too much for him.

'A violent storm raged within me,' he says, 'bringing with it a flood of tears,' and he retired into a still more solitary place. Rising once more he flung himself under a fig tree in an agony of remorse, exclaiming, 'How long, O Lord, how long? Remember not my former sins! Tomorrow and tomorrow and tomorrow—why not now? Why should there not be in this hour an end of my baseness?'

In the midst of his agitated prayer he heard the voice of a child, whether boy or girl he knew not, singing again and again the words, '*Tolle, lege; tolle, lege*'—'Take, read; take, read.' Believing this to be a divine intimation, he began intently to consider whether those words were ever used in any childish game. Feeling sure that he had never heard them used by children in their play, he repressed his tears, and took the voice to mean that God bade him to open a book and read the first verse on which he lighted. He had heard from Pontitianus how Antony's life had been practically decided by these *sortes Biblicae*, when he had understood as a direct command to himself the words of the gospel—'Go, sell everything you have and give to the poor.' He rushed back to the place in which he had left Alypius sitting, for there he had laid down the manuscript of St Paul.

'I seized it, opened it, and read in silence the verse on which my eyes first fell—"Not in orgies and drunkenness, not in sexual immorality and debauchery, not in dissension and jealousy. Rather, clothe yourselves with the Lord Jesus Christ, and do not think about how to gratify the desires of the sinful nature" (Romans 13:13–14). I wished to read no more. There was no need. For instantly, as though the light of salvation had been poured into my heart with the close of this sentence, all the darkness of my doubts had fled away.'

The Latin church only celebrates *two* conversions—those of St Paul (Jan. 25), and St Augustine (May 5).

Putting his finger in the place, he closed the volume, and, with a countenance which had resumed its calm, he indicated to Alypius how things stood with him. Alypius then implied that he too had been changed. He asked to see what Augustine had read, and on being shown the passage he called his friend's attention to the words which followed—'Accept him whose faith is weak' (Romans 14:1).

Those words confirmed him, for he applied them to himself, although, says Augustine, he had long been far his superior in moral character. They went to Monnica and told her what had occurred. She recognised that God, in answer to her prayers, had granted her even more than she had ever dared to hope. For,

> Now the sweet arrow of the love divine,
>   Remorselessly had pierced Augustine's heart;
> The flowers of speech he will no more entwine,
>   Frequent no more the rhetorician's mart:
> He gazeth on the sun so long denied,
> And the sun-gazer groweth sunny-eyed.

5

Cassiciacum

Augustine now determined to abandon the profession of rhetoric, which he could hardly persuade himself to retain even for the twenty days which intervened before the vintage holiday naturally closed the term. He wished neither to make a sensation nor to offend the parents of his pupils, and he was able to offer the perfectly true excuse that some disease of the chest was severely trying him, and that at least a temporary rest was indispensable. But, in point of fact, he was a changed man, and could not bear any longer to be a 'seller of words'. The determination to be pure had triumphed in him, and he now saw that by God's grace this was possible. The desire for earthly gain and earthly glory was altogether dead.

The purpose of Augustine to retire and devote his life wholly to God was only known to a few friends. Among these was Verecundus, a grammarian of Milan, but not yet a Christian, to whom he was deeply attached, and who was unable to join the new converts because he was married to a faithful wife, whom he loved, and with whom they advised him to stay. Nebridius, who mainly out of kindness assisted him in his school, intended soon to attach himself to their party. When Augustine wrote his *Confessions* both Nebridius and Verecundus were dead. Both had been baptised before their death, and Nebridius, who was then a Docetist, gave up his error, was baptised shortly after Augustine, and brought over his whole family to the Christian faith.

Verecundus rendered to Augustine and his friends the great service of lending them his country house, which bore the name of Cassiciacum, for which Augustine prays that God may reward him. It was a pleasant villa in the mountains, amid chestnuts and olives and vineyards and fields of harvest, not far from the Lago Maggiore, surrounded by a shady garden and green meadows, which were watered by a little stream. Thither Augustine went, in the autumn of 386, with a very peaceful and joyous heart, accompanied by his mother Monnica, his brother Navigius, his pupils Trygetius and Licentius, his cousins Lastidianus and Rusticus, his friend Alypius, and Adeodatus, then a boy of fifteen, the son of his sin.

Navigius, Lastidianus and Rusticus, being men of no great knowledge or capacity, took very little part in the discussions in which Augustine and Alypius were the chief disputants, and which were meant to stimulate the two youths in the power of impromptu expression and philosophic reasoning. Trygetius was a young soldier who had left the army and entered keenly into questions of deep and abstract interest. The young Licentius, 'the laureate of the little band', a son of Romanianus, was abler than his companion, but was distracted by his passion for poetry, and, fired by their readings of Virgil, had begun a poem on Pyramus and Thisbe. His complimentary poem to his beloved teacher is still extant.

At Cassiciacum they lived in delightful peace, and we are glad to get so clear a glimpse of the daily life of that beautiful but humble society. Monnica undertook for them the management of the household. Augustine's time was fully occupied. He rose with the dawn. He studied the Psalms with inexpressible pleasure. He took his share in rustic toil, and superintended the labourers. Much of the day was spent in this work, in writing letters, and in teaching his

pupils. Half of the night was always devoted to meditations. The meals were few, brief, and extremely simple,
but they were brightened by genial fellowship. They used
all to combine in the discussion of some grave and important subject, and his two pupils made an advance so won-
derful as to be almost incredible to those who had previ-
ously known them. At these discussions a shorthand writer
was always present, and they form the substance of the
books *Against the Academicians, On the Order of Providence,*
and *On a Happy Life.* The writer reported the exact words
of Augustine and Alypius, and the substance of the
remarks of the others. Augustine disliked the physical
labour of writing, and was not in sufficiently good health
to undertake it.

The work known as *Against the Academicians* is of no great
value. It simply reports the discussions of three days as to
the attainability of truth. Augustine admits that it might
have been compressed into much smaller space than three
books if it had not been his object to train the powers of the
young men. The discussion *On a Happy Life* also occupied
three days, and is designed to prove that true happiness
consists in knowing God. The two books *On Order* are a
sort of theodicy.

Another product of the seven-months' stay at Cassiciacum
is the *Soliloquia,* in which, in the ecstasy of holy contemplation, he discusses the loftiest problems with God and with
his own soul. These books have not yet attained the specifi-
cally Christian character of his later writings. He confesses
that they breathe more of the cedars of the gymnasia,
which God has broken, than the wholesome herbage of the
church, which is fatal to serpents.

Alypius had expressly urged him not to introduce the
name of Christ into these discussions, because he wished
them to be purely philosophical in their character. And yet
they rest on a Christian basis, and have a certain charm of
their own. The sharers in the philosophic enquiry are no
longer the splendid statesmen and orators whose words

breathe and burn in the eloquent pages of Cicero, nor do they converse in the magnificent villas adorned with statues of heathen philosophers or heathen gods. They are humble provincial neophytes, talking with young Christian pupils, under the wintry sunshine in the rustic garden or humble bathroom of a country farm.

What can be more delightful in its simplicity than the narrative of the trivial incident which gave rise to the discussion *On Order*?

It was late autumn, and the nights were long. Since even wealthy Italians were unable to afford the luxury of lamps for all the hours of darkness, Augustine accustomed himself to lie awake in meditation for the first or last half of every night. He had tried to train his pupils also in this habit of thinking, that they might not spend too much time exclusively over books, but might also accustom their minds to dwell at home. Augustine, then, was lying awake, when his attention was attracted by the intermittent gushes of the little stream which fed the bath. He could not understand why its music as it ran over the pebbles was sometimes low and sometimes loud. While trying to imagine the reason, he found that Licentius also was lying awake, for he knocked on the floor with a stick beside his bed to frighten away some troublesome mice.

'Licentius,' said Augustine, '—for I see that your muse has kindled a light for your lucubrations—have you noticed how unevenly that water-channel is sounding?'

'That,' he answered, 'is nothing at all new to me. For in my longing for fair weather, when I awoke and had listened intently lest a shower should be coming on, the water was gushing in the same way as now.'

'Yes,' said Trygetius, 'I noticed it too';—and thus showed that he also, without their knowing it, was lying awake in his bed.

Augustine thought that the opportunity should not be thrown away, so he asked his pupils what they took to be the reason for the phenomenon, for at that hour no one could be either crossing the stream or washing anything in it. Licentius replied that it was caused by the dense fall of the autumn leaves, which alternately impeded, and were swept away by, the flow of the water.

> I seem to hear
> The very leaf which autumn-tide brought low
> In Lombardy a thousand years ago,
> And as it dropped insubstantive on the rill,
> And, sinking, helped to break the brimming flow,
> Set moving high discourse of fate and will,
> Proving that chance is God's incognito;
> That Chance, in heaven's tongue Order, interweaves
> Vaster variety than waves and leaves.

Augustine thought he was right, and praised him for his acuteness, confessing that he himself had been unable to conjecture the cause. A little afterwards he added, 'You were right not to wonder, and to keep yourself at home with your Calliope.'

'Yes,' said Licentius; 'but you have now given me a great cause for wonder.'

'What is that?' asked Augustine.

'Why,' answered the youth, 'that *you* wondered at such things.'

'Why should I not wonder?' asked Augustine; 'the vice of wonder is caused by something unusual, beyond the obvious order of causes.'

'Beyond what is obvious, I admit,' said Licentius; 'but nothing seems to me to happen beyond the true order of things.'

'Excellent,' exclaimed Augustine, surprised at the readiness and acuteness of the remark; 'you are getting far higher than the Helicon, to whose summit, as though to heaven, you are striving to attain. But pray support the opinion, for I shall try to shake it.'

'Please leave me alone,' he replied; 'I am thinking other things.'

Fearing from this that his poetic studies would alienate Licentius from the philosophy, which was more important, Augustine complained that he was vexed at the youth's incessant pursuit of verse, which was building a more cruel wall between him and the truth than his verse was trying to build a wall between Pyramus and Thisbe—for that wall had at least a chink in it.

Licentius made no answer, and Augustine returned to his own meditations, thinking it useless to disturb the mind of his pupil, which was so much preoccupied. But after a pause Licentius quoted a line of Terence—

By my own testimony I am as wretched as a mouse.

'I think,' he added, 'that could be said of me; but the "today I am undone," which follows, shall not be true of me. I hope you won't disdain to take a lesson from mice, as the superstitious are wont to do: if I by my knocking warned the mouse (who betrayed to you that I was awake) that he should be wise and go and be quiet in his hole, why should not I, by the sound of your voice, be warned to philosophise rather than to sing? For philosophy is, as you have begun to persuade me, our true and unshaken home. So then, if it does not trouble you, ask what you wish. I will do my best to defend the order of things, and will assert that nothing can occur beyond their order. And if you vanquish me in the disputation I shall not attribute it to anything accidental, but to the order of things.'

Trygetius assented to the proposal, and after he had chaffed Licentius a little for abandoning his Academic 'suspension of judgement' by such positive assertions, the discussion began.

Again, what could be more naïvely simple than the renewal of the talk after the day had dawned? Augustine indirectly reminds Licentius how Monnica had reproved him the previous night for singing the verse of a psalm— of which he had just learnt the tune—in a place and at a time which she considered unsuitable. Thus the dialogue springs up from the most trivial daily incidents. But the chief value of these discussions is that they uplift every question to the highest conclusion. 'The philosophy conducts to religion, and the two are there united.'

We may notice further points of interest in these early works.

One is the beautiful insight exhibited in the answers of Monnica, whose want of knowledge and philosophy was amply supplemented by her saintly experience. When they were discussing a happy life, she said, 'If a man wishes and possesses good things, he is happy; if he wishes for bad things, he is wretched even if he possesses them.'

'If a man be possessed of every source of earthly felicity,' she said, 'he still could not be satisfied with them, and therefore would always be wretched because he would always be in want. No one, therefore, can be made happy by those things, but only by moderation of mind.'

She compared the ever-wavering Academics to persons who had the epilepsy, and said, 'To be in want is to be wretched; and if a man is in want of wisdom he is a far greater pauper than if he is in want of money.'

She closed the discussion *On a Happy Life* by quoting the hymn of Ambrose, 'Fove precantes, Trinitas', adding that 'the happy life, the perfect life, was that to which we could be gradually led by firm faith, by cheerful hope, by burning charity.'

Monnica sat beside them, says Augustine, 'in the dress indeed of a woman, but with the faith of a man, the calmness of old age, the love of a mother, and the holiness of a Christian'. It is perhaps surprising that he should express such rapturous admiration at the expression of truths which had long been the commonplaces of Plato and the Stoics, of Cicero and of Seneca; but what seemed so admirable was that the loftiest morality of the greatest heathen thinkers had become the ordinary heritage of the most uninstructed Christians. 'What had been a rare heroism had become an everyday belief,' so that

> Each little voice in turn
> Some glorious truth proclaims,
> What sages would have died to learn
> Now taught by cottage dames.

What a new touch of Christian enthusiasm and tenderness is introduced into even the most jejune of these discussions when we read that the rhetorician, now a poor neophyte, prayed and shed tears when he thought of the coming discussion of the day, and of the ardour of his young pupils for the solution of such lofty problems! The sensibility of his genius is inspired by the sincerity of his love to God and of his desire to do his duty to men.

The gifted boy Adeodatus also distinguished himself in these philosophical discussions, and his very words are often reported. Augustine shuddered at the precocious promise of his son's intellect, lest it should portend an early death.

He had asked, 'Who is in possession of God?'

Licentius said, 'He who lives well'; Trygetius, 'He who does what God wills'; but the boy said, 'He who has not an impure spirit', and Monnica and Navigius agreed with him.

When his father asked him to define what he meant, he said, 'He has not an impure spirit who lives chastely.'

'And whom do you call chaste; a man who commits no sins or a man who is free from impurity?'

'How,' answered Adeodatus, 'can he be chaste, who, though pure, is yet enslaved by other sins? He lives chastely who attends wholly to the will of God, and holds himself firm to him alone.' These definitions prefaced the discussion *On a Happy Life*, which was held on Augustine's birthday in the bathroom of the little villa.

Augustine also gives us an interesting story about his two pupils. The stimulating method which he adopted with them naturally awoke in them a spirit of emulation and even of occasional rivalry, and all the more from the very unusual circumstance that their arguments were taken down and published.

At one point the discussion *On Order* was broken rather painfully by a quarrel between the disputants. In the heat of discussion Trygetius had been led to say that 'when we say "God", we usually think of the Father, and that we think of Christ when we say "the Son of God".'

'A fine thing truly,' said Licentius; 'shall we then deny that the Son of God is God?'

Trygetius hesitated, but replied, 'He is indeed God, yet properly we call the Father God.'

'Stop!' said Augustine; 'for the Son is also properly called God.'

Trygetius felt a little horrified at his implied distinction, and as the shorthand writer was taking everything down as usual, he begged that his remark might not be reported. Licentius, however, as is the way with boys—or rather, alas! with all human beings—urged that the remark of Trygetius should be left undeleted—'as though the question were being discussed among us only for the sake of glory!'

Augustine thereupon reproved him in terms so severe that he blushed, and then it was the turn of Trygetius to laugh and exult. Augustine was grieved to the heart. 'Is this your conduct?' he exclaimed. 'Does not the thought of the mass of vices and the darkness of ignorance, with which we are oppressed and covered, influence you? Is this that earnestness and desire for divine truth in you at which a little while ago I foolishly rejoiced? Oh, if you could see, even with such purblind eyes as I do, in what perils we are lying, what madness of disease that laughter of yours implies! Unhappy boys! Know you not where we are? . . . Do not, I entreat you, double my sorrows. If you owe me anything, if you willingly call me Master, give me my reward—be good!'

He ended with a burst of tears, but Licentius, indignant that all this had been written down, said somewhat pertly,

'Why, what have we done, pray?'

'What!' exclaimed Augustine; 'do you not even confess your fault? Do you not know how angry I used to be in my school when boys, out of vainglory, declaimed compositions which were not their own to gain applause? I thought that *you* had risen to higher feelings.'

'You shall find out how much better we shall be in future,' said the penitent boy, 'but I entreat you by everything you love to pardon us, and order all that has passed to be blotted out of the notes.'

'Nay,' said Trygentius; 'let our punishment abide, that the very fame which allures us may terrify us from loving her by her own scourge, for we shall do our very utmost to prevent these pages from getting into the hands of any but our friends and intimates.'

In that expectation the boys were mistaken, for, instead of being known only to their own little circle, their boyish faults, enshrined in the writings which have been preserved because of the splendour of their tutor's reputation, have become known to all subsequent ages.

But the incident is full of human interest, and strikingly illustrates the method of education which Augustine adopted, the warmth and depth of his feelings, and the lofty standard which he always kept before the eyes of those who had been entrusted to his care.

Augustine tells us two other incidents of these days. The one was how he cured himself of a habit which had become almost inveterate of taking oaths about everything—henceforth he only appealed to the witness of God on solemn occasions, which he justified by the example of St Paul. The other was that, during a part of this happy time, he suffered from agonies of toothache—or more probably neuralgia—so severe that he was even unable to speak, and could scarcely even think. He thought that by more thoroughly contemplating the splendour of truth he could either dispel the pain, or at any rate endure it more easily; but at last his torture was so great that he took a writing tablet and wrote on it an entreaty that all who were present would pray for him. They had scarcely knelt down when, not only to the astonishment but almost to the alarm of Augustine, the pain instantly ceased. He had never before had so remarkable an experience, and it increased the humble faith and hope with which he was contemplating his approaching baptism.

For he had scarcely arrived at Cassiciacum before he wrote to Ambrose telling him something of his story, and offering himself as a candidate for baptism. He was now therefore a member of the class of *competentes*, and Alypius and Adeodatus were to be baptised with him. He had also asked Ambrose which of the books of scripture he had better read with special attention. Ambrose suggested the book of Isaiah. Augustine began it, but finding himself unable to understand the earlier chapters, he postponed the study to some time when he should be better able to grasp the meaning.

It will be seen, in the whole remaining course of Augustine's life, that, after his conversion, he was indeed a man whose heart had been changed by the grace of God. He was converted, and his one desire was thenceforth to strengthen his brethren. But we must not fall into the error of supposing that he had no more spiritual battles to win, no results of past delinquency to conquer with the whole effort of his soul, and by constantly seeking for the grace of God.

The wounds were healed, the scars remained. He felt for many a year the reactions and after-workings of the second and evil nature which habit had induced. He still sometimes felt 'the infernal fire of lust' leaping up from its white embers in his heart. His nightly dreams were still disturbed with temptations which he had conquered in his waking hours.

'Am I not,' he cries, 'am I not in dreams the man I am, O Lord my God? Does my reason slumber as well as the senses of my body? Cannot thy mighty hand purify the weakness of my soul, and with richer grace exterminate the guiltiness of my dreams? Yea, thou wilt more and more extend to me thy gifts, that my soul may follow thee, and even in my dreams may be beside thee, full of purity, since thou canst do more than we ask or understand.' The tenth book of his *Confessions* shows us the hard and continuous struggle which he was still forced to maintain, and we hear him lament that evil still clung to him, not only in his dreams, but even in his religious exercises.

6

After Baptism

The happy days of Cassiciacum—perhaps the happiest in Augustine's life—drew rapidly to a close, and the little band of friends had to leave that quiet scene with all its enchanting serenity and verdure, to plunge once more into the troubled stream of active life. It is never possible to linger for long among the sheepfolds, listening to the bleating of the sheep, or to gaze on the bright countenance of truth in the dewy air of delightful studies.

The chief time for baptism was Easter, and those who desired to join the preparation classes of *competentes* gave in their names at the beginning of Lent. Both Augustine and Alypius returned to Milan, and were diligent and humble pupils of the catechists, though both were probably superior to their teachers alike in learning, ability, and devoted faithfulness. In accordance with the ascetic tendencies of the day they both lived on a very small quantity of the plainest food, and Alypius used sometimes to walk barefooted even when the ground was hard with frost.

During these days Augustine wrote his book *On the Immortality of the Soul*, by way of supplement to his *Soliloquies*, and began his work on the elements of a liberal education, of which the books on music were afterwards finished. The earlier part of this book is arid and unimportant, but he gradually leads up from aesthetics to religion.

On Easter Eve, 387—a day specially set apart for the baptism of adults—Augustine was baptised with Alypius and his young son Adeodatus, who was but fifteen years old, but whose gifts and graces were such as to fit him for receiving that solemn sacrament. The scene doubtless resembled that which he has described as occurring at the baptism of Victorinus, as the two young men and the boy entered the deep font on Holy Saturday, 387, were thrice plunged beneath the lustral wave, and went forth in their white chrisom robes. Augustine has not detailed the incidents of the day, but we know how deeply he was affected, even to tears, by the sweet sound of psalms and hymns sung by the congregation.

Henceforth the one object of Augustine was to give himself heart and soul to God. He and his friends now desired to live as monks. He does not indeed apply the name *monachus* to himself, but he applied it to Albina, Pinianus, and Melania, when they were living in Africa in a manner like his own.

Not long after his baptism he went with Monnica, his younger brother Navigius, Alypius, and Adeodatus to Ostia, determined to return to Africa, and there to find some suitable spot for founding a coenobitic community of ten persons, for whom two were, in turn, to be purveyors. They were joined by Evodius of Tagaste, a young army officer who a little before had abandoned his profession and been baptised.

At Ostia they refreshed themselves for their long journey, and made all their preparations to bid a final farewell to the country in which a stay of three years had altered the whole destiny of their lives. Ostia was then a busy and prosperous port, very unlike 'the desolate ruins by the Yellow Tiber on which the traveller now gazes, shortly after passing from the trees and violet-tufted hedgerows of the Campagna, over the vast marsh and by the salt-pits, looking to the sombre belt of pine by Castel Fugano'. But the little party of Roman Africans found there some quiet resting-place where they were able to recruit their strength after the fatigues of their journey, and to prepare for the stormy passage from Italy to Carthage.

One evening Augustine and his mother were sitting at a window which looked over the little garden of their house. They were alone, and Monnica, who then seemed to be in perfect health, little thought that in five or six days she would be dead. As they leaned on the window-sill under the unclouded starlight, looking over the garden and the sea, the sweet and solemn stillness of the hour attuned their thoughts to holy things. They talked together of the kingdom of God, and of the way in which men may get rid of earthly temptations and lusts by abandoning them and occupying the soul with sacred aspirations. The mother and son raised their whole hearts to heaven, until they seemed to have left all earthly thoughts behind, and enjoyed a foretaste of the hour when the faithful shall enter into the joy of their Lord.

'My son,' said Monnica, before they parted, 'as far as I am concerned, nothing in this life delights me any longer. What I am to do here, or why I am here, I know not, since for me the hope of this world is spent. There was but one reason why I desired to linger in this life a little longer. It was that I might see you a Catholic Christian before I died. My God has granted me this in more abundant measure, so that I even see you his servant, despising all earthly felicity. What do I here?'

Augustine, like Basil, enjoyed with an almost modern keenness the glories of nature, and the sea always affected him with peculiar delight and awe. In the *City of God*, he speaks of 'the multiform and various loveliness of sky, and earth, and sea; the magnificent spectacle even of the sea alone, when it clothes itself with various colours as with robes, and is sometimes green, and that in many fashions, and sometimes purple, and sometimes azure'. He even speaks of a deeper delight in watching its agitation. Never could he have gazed over the twilight waves with higher and holier feelings than on this memorable evening.

About five days after this happy talk Monnica was seized with a fever, and fell into a long swoon. When she awoke she saw her two sons standing by her bed, and asked, 'Where am I?' Gazing at them as they stood, dumb with grief, she said, 'Will you bury your mother here?'

Navigius, knowing that it had been her wish to be laid in the same grave as her husband Patricius, said, 'It would have been a happier thing for you to die at home.'

She looked first at him and then at Augustine, and said, 'See what he says!' Then she added, 'My sons, bury this body where you will; do not trouble yourselves about it. I ask of you this only—remember me whenever you come to God's altar.'

A few days earlier, when Augustine was not present, she had been talking with his friends about the contempt of life and the blessing of death, and on being asked whether she would not dread to leave her body so far from her own country, she answered, 'Nothing is afar from God; nor need I fear lest he, at the end of the world, should forget whence he should raise me from the dead.'

On the ninth day of her illness, in the fifty-sixth year of her age, that faithful and holy soul was set free from her mortal body. Augustine was then thirty-three.

He closed her eyes in deep sadness, and his tears began to flow. He repressed them by a strong effort of his will, feeling that there was nothing there for tears. The boy Adeodatus began to wail aloud, but he was checked by those who were present, who thought it unfitting for men with Christian hopes that such a death should be celebrated by groans and lamentations, when they knew that to God's children death is the great birthright of the redeemed. Then Evodius took up a Psalter, and together they chanted the psalm,

> I will sing of your love and justice;
> to you, O LORD, I will sing praise.   (Psalm 101:1)

Augustine was grieved all the more because he found it impossible to conquer his own natural grief, and put upon himself so violent a strain that he went and returned to the funeral without a tear. Not knowing how to crush his misery, he went to the bath, having been told that this would drive away his anguish; but he found it of no avail. A night's sleep refreshed him, and when he awoke in the morning he recalled the beautiful hymn of Ambrose—

> Creator of the earth and sky,
> Ruling the firmament on high,
> Clothing the day with robes of light,
> Blessing with gracious sleep the night,
>
> That rest may comfort weary men,
> And brace to useful toil again,
> And soothe awhile the harassed mind,
> And sorrow's heavy load unbind.

And then at last, as he thought of the beautiful life which he was no longer to witness, he gave himself to tears for her and for himself, which no eye witnessed but that of God. Strange that he should have felt it necessary to apologise, to regard it almost as a sin to be confessed, that he should have wept for the short space of an hour for the mother who had so often wept for him!

The death of Monnica disconcerted the plans of the friends, and they put off the journey to Africa. For about a year Augustine lived at Rome. Now that he had abandoned his professorial duties he had leisure to write. During this year he wrote his two books, *On the Morals of Manicheans* and *On the Morals of the Catholic Church*. His twofold object was to show that the boasted continence of the Manichees was unreal, and that their criticisms of the Old Testament were founded on ignorance, whereas the church presented a glorious example of virtue in the lives of her hermits, coenobites, and bishops. In the glowing eulogy of the church we see the germ of the views afterwards developed in the Donatist controversy, as well as those on the union of revelation with reason, and authority with faith, on which he always insisted.

He also wrote his book *On the 'Quantity' of the Soul*. In this book occurs the characteristic sentence, 'God is not only the creator, but the native-land of the soul,' with which Villemain compares the expression of Malebranche, 'God is the place of spirits, as space is the place of bodies.' With this again we may compare the name 'Place' given to God by some of the Rabbis, and the remark that 'God is not in place but place in God.'

Here also Augustine began his book *On Free Will*, which was used by Pelagius as expressing his own views. As a specimen of the dialectical skill of Augustine we may quote this passage:

> Will would neither be ours, nor will at all, if it was not in our power. If then it is in our power we are free to use it; whence it follows that, without disputing the entire foreknowledge of God, we will what we will. If he foreknows our will it must be will that he foreknows, for it is a will which he has foreseen, and could not be a will if it were not in our power. He therefore equally foresaw this power. His foreknowledge does not deprive me of the power which it has infallibly foreseen.

After the death of Monnica we lose the help of the *Confessions*, of which the tenth and following books cease to be autobiographical and are occupied with philosophical, spiritual, and exegetical reflections.

7

Monk

After a year spent at Rome in profitable studies, Augustine
sailed to Carthage, where he was a guest in the house of
Innocentius, a former agent of the Praetor of Africa. He
was here an eyewitness of an event which he regarded as
directly miraculous. Innocentius, a man who feared God
with all his house, had been afflicted with fistulas, and had
undergone the protracted agony of several operations.
One of these was a deep fistula which remained after the
others were healed. His own private physician had told
him that this also would require an operation, but the
other doctors, who had treated the domestic practitioner
with contempt, and had not even allowed him to witness
their operations, soothed Innocentius with hopes and
promises, which were confirmed by an aged and distinguished leader of the profession named Ammonius, whom
they had called into consultation. Innocentius, imagining
himself secure, had laughed at his domestic doctor, but at
last the physicians had been compelled to come round to
his opinion, and to announce that, after all, another operation would be necessary.

Innocentius in an access of anger and horror drove
them all from his presence, and refused to see them again.
He was therefore compelled to send for an Alexandrian
surgeon of the highest eminence, who, after seeing him,

acted in the honourable way for which so many members of that great profession are distinguished, and refused to reap the laurels of the cure which, now that only one more operation was necessary, really belonged to his professional brethren. They were recalled, and the Alexandrian promised to assist at the operation, which was postponed till the following day.

After they had gone, a wail of distress filled the house, for Innocentius dreaded the anguish of the knife even more than the death which he felt convinced would result from it. Uzalensis, the Bishop of Tagaste, his future successor Aurelius, and with them a presbyter and a deacon, came in the evening to pay him their usual daily visit of consolation. He implored them to pray for him, and when they knelt on their knees he prostrated himself on his face with a violent movement, and began to pour forth his prayers to God with floods of tears, and with sobs and groans which shook his whole frame, and almost choked his words. Whether the others prayed Augustine cannot tell, but he was himself so much absorbed in what Innocentius was doing that he could not pray himself. He could only briefly exclaim in his heart, 'O Lord, what prayers of thy people hearest thou, if thou hearest not these?' for it seemed that nothing could be added to such entreaties unless Innocentius died while praying. They rose; the bishop gave his blessing; Innocentius entreated them to be present with him the next morning.

The dreaded day dawned; they came; the physicians were present; the terrible surgical implements were produced before their horror-stricken eyes; the unhappy patient was bound down in the requisite position. The ligaments were untied; the place was laid bare; the chief physician examined it with his knife in his hand. They scrutinised it; handled it; tried it in every possible way. No fistula was there! It was entirely healed, and nothing remained but a solid scar! Augustine says that the joy which followed, the tears of congratulation, the thanksgivings to the God of power and mercy, must be imagined rather than described.

Augustine left Carthage for Tagaste, and there he sold his paternal estate and gave the whole proceeds to the poor, reserving nothing for himself, that he might serve God with unimpeded soul. We are told again and again of a similar step being taken by the devoted Christians of this period, and we would gladly have been informed wherein this 'giving to the poor' consisted. So far as the money was spent in founding institutions for the support of virtuous indigence, or the cure of sickness, it was wisely spent; but there is reason to fear that the institutions of the day fostered an aimless and promiscuous almsgiving, which, while it seemed to obey the letter of scripture, was in deadly opposition to its spirit. To give thus indiscriminately was to foster the curse of mendicant pauperism, and to inflict a grievous injury not only upon society in general, but most of all upon the recipients of a blind and unreasoning bounty. 'Blessed is he that *considereth* the poor,' and such consideration has long led every wise Christian to see that no almsgiving to the poor is true charity which does not elevate while it relieves—nay, that it is not charity but injury to give when the giving only helps to multiply the number of thriftless, idle, and vicious lives. The distributions of the third and fourth centuries, the monastic doles of the Middle Ages, were a fruitful source of demoralisation and misery. In what sense and in what way Augustine, and the friends whom he induced to follow his example, sold all they had and gave to the poor we do not know. In any case they had the full merit of their holy self-sacrifice. It would be absurd to blame them, because they had not anticipated the lessons which have been taught us by the experience of so many hundred years.

But though the views of Augustine on the subject of almsgiving may have been as little in accordance with the teaching of political economy as those of his own and many subsequent ages, we are glad to find that he did not share the extravagant misconceptions which prevailed among many of the early ascetics. When the Pelagians wished to exclude from the kingdom of heaven the rich who did not part with their goods, he explained to them that the call to do this was not uttered to all men. It was only 'a counsel of perfection' to those who received and who needed it, nor was it given to the rich only. If he mentions that he himself has obeyed the command of Christ to the young ruler, he only does so to show that he is not pleading his own cause; and he adds that he was not a rich man any more than the apostles were.

The little community occupied as tenants the patrimonial house and estate near the walls of Tagaste which Augustine might have occupied as an owner. Alypius, Romanianus, and Evodius were already with him; now he was joined by Severus, afterwards Bishop of Mileum, and others both rich and poor. In this monastic retreat he spent three peaceful but busy years. They were much occupied in the study of scripture, and it was in response to the constant enquiries of his companions that Augustine dictated the answers which afterwards made up the book of eighty-three questions. He also kept up an animated correspondence with Nebridius until his early death, and gave all the help he could to those who consulted him about their civil concerns. He wrote two books on Genesis against the Manicheans, in which he adopted the allegoric method of interpretation; twelve books on the literal interpretation, which he never completed; six books on music, about the value of which, except the sixth book, he seems himself to have had grave doubts, but which illustrate his way of mingling every topic with aspiration towards God; two books on the Master, containing a discussion with Adeodatus, in which he tries to lead him to see that the one great teacher is God; and his valuable treatise on true religion.

By these writings, and by his holy life, he became widely famous. Coenobitic communities were until that time almost wholly unknown in Africa, and it was only from his example that they became, in a short time, extremely numerous. He could not but be aware that if he entered any city where there was no bishop, he ran considerable risk of being seized by force, and consecrated to the episcopal office. He therefore sedulously avoided such places. But towards the end of his three years he was invited to Hippo Regius by a friend, who had been one of the Imperial Commissioners, who told him that he felt a strong inclination to sell all that he had and join him in his monastery if only he would come and teach him. Augustine came, but his friend postponed his determination from day to day.

Hippo Regius—so called to distinguish it from another Hippo—was a fortified city of great distinction, and the capital of the district of maritime Numidia in which it stood. The poet Statius calls it 'Hippo, beloved by ancient kings'. Nothing now remains of it except a few ruined cisterns near the modern town of Bona, and the mouth of the river Reybouse. One of its bishops, named Theogenes, had been a martyr in the days of Cyprian, and it could boast of twenty martyrs besides. The Christian basilica was one of the most conspicuous ornaments of the city. But Augustine thought himself safe at Hippo, because it was under the presidency of an excellent bishop named Valerius, who stood at the head of a considerable number of chorepiscopi (or suffragan bishops).

But Valerius was advancing in years, and, being a Greek, could not preach in Latin as fluently as he desired. He had long been praying that God would grant him the co-operation of some pious and competent presbyter to assist him in his labours, and he rejoiced at the opportunity which now offered itself of securing the support of the foremost among the African Christians. Augustine, suspecting nothing, went to service in the church, and stood among the common multitude. But they knew his history; and when Valerius began to preach about the necessity of ordaining a presbyter to assist him, they seized Augustine, and with loud shouts demanded that he should be ordained. Dreading the labours to which he would be exposed in a church already rent with schism, he protested against their purpose with floods of tears, which they attributed to the fact that he was only to be ordained a presbyter and not a bishop! The multitude sometimes claimed the ordination of a man by whose wealth they could be assisted, or protected by his power; but Augustine was a simple layman, with no office, no gold or silver, who possessed nothing but the clothes in which he stood. They showed insight in their demand. Had it not been for the fame of Augustine, the name of Hippo would have been absolutely unknown.

Feeling himself unable to resist—regarding the voices of the people as a call of God—Augustine reluctantly submitted to ordination. But the events had been so sudden that he begged Valerius to give him leave of absence till the following Easter, that by prayer and meditation and study of the scriptures he might prepare himself for his sacred duties. The letter in which he pleaded with Valerius for this remission is a beautiful proof both of his humility and of his sense of the grandeur of the office to which he was henceforth to devote his life.

So ended the quiet time at Tagaste, which had only been embittered by the loss of his friend Nebridius, and of his young and deeply beloved Adeodatus, who was cut off in the blossom of his age before he had had time to fulfil the brilliant promise of his intellect. Augustine speaks but little of this bereavement, for Adeodatus was the son of his shame, and he confesses that he has no share in that bright young soul except his sin. But there are many signs that the death of this fine boy caused him the deepest sorrow.

He returned to Hippo at the Easter of 391, in the fortieth year of his age. Valerius received him with warm affection, and as he felt no jealousy towards his presbyter, the two lived and worked together in beautiful concord.

Augustine, writing to the Donatist Bishop of Hippo in the absence of Valerius, is able to assure him that Valerius will approve of any step taken by himself. He always spoke of him with reverence and affection, and tells an anecdote of the old man's naïve delight when, on hearing the word *salus* constantly used by two Punic rustics, he asked them what the word meant, and was told that it meant 'three'; so that the Latin word for salvation was the Punic word for the Trinity.

Valerius felt such confidence in Augustine that he even appointed him to preach in his place and in his presence. This was contrary to the custom of the African church, where, according to a rule which Jerome condemns as due to jealousy, bishops did not allow their presbyters to preach. Valerius was blamed for his innovation, but such was the fame of Augustine's sermons that the custom soon spread into the other churches of Africa.

Knowing the yearning of Augustine for the monastic life, Valerius gave him a garden contiguous to the church, where he erected a building suitable to his purpose. The rule of the house was that the brethren who lived in it should, like Augustine himself, sell all that they had, whether it was much or little, and give to the poor. No distinction was made among them in favour of previous rank or wealth, but they aimed at reproducing the life of the little primitive church in Jerusalem, by having all things in common. They were to call nothing their own. The monastery at Hippo became a training-school for the clergy, and furnished no less than ten bishops to the church of Africa. Among the more illustrious of these were Alypius of Tagaste, Profuturus of Cirta, the Metropolitan of Numidia, Severus of Mileum, and Possidius of Calama. The latter enjoyed the friendship of Augustine for forty years, and was peculiarly fitted to become his biographer, for during that long period no shadow of dissension ever arose between them.

The pupils of Augustine disseminated far and wide in

their dioceses and parishes his monastic institutions. They were not looked upon by all as an unmixed benefit, and Augustine himself found by bitter experience that the monk's dress may easily conceal the heart of the hypocrite and the libertine. He confesses that even in his own house there were good monks and there were bad monks. He could not hope, he said, to make it purer than Noah's ark; or than the little band of apostles, of whom one was a Judas; or than heaven, from which the angels fell. Some of the best men whom he had ever known had been trained in monasteries, but also some of the worst.

He makes this confession on the occasion of a frightful scandal which arose in his community from the charges made against each other by a priest named Bonifacius and a layman named Spes. It was impossible to discover which of the two was really guilty, and after much anguish of mind Augustine saw no better way to decide the question than to send them both to the grave of St Felix at Nola in order that there the innocence or the guilt of each might be decided by some miraculous intervention.

On another occasion a monk pleaded fatalism as an excuse both for disobedience and for immorality. Donatus and his brother left the monastery in order to push their ambitious views elsewhere. Paulus, Bishop of Cataqua, disgraced the church of Hippo by his misconduct, and Augustine had to renounce his communion. Antonius had been trained in the house from his earliest boyhood, and at last Augustine recommended him for the bishopric of Fussala; but he so completely disgraced his office that Augustine half determined to resign the see of Hippo to testify his penitence for having supported the claims of such a man. Another monk whom he had known from childhood fell grievously away in spite of every effort which he could make to save him.

Augustine pleads that it was impossible to know the real character of men until they had been actually admitted into the house, so that no human power could prevent the falling away of some. Others, who entered in the hope of finding a harbour of refuge, felt so bitterly disappointed when they discovered that there were bad brethren in the monastery as well as bad men in the world, that they abandoned their vows in disgust, and became, if not the calumniators, yet the uncharitable critics, of institutions which had failed to satisfy an unreasonable ideal. The mixture of classes among the brethren, the free admission of husbandmen, artisans, slaves, and paupers, rendered it more difficult to secure perfect sanctity, or even the absence of grave abuses. Among so many it was inevitable that some should be brought thither by the dubious motives which also crowded the monasteries with so many worthless characters during the Middle Ages.

> 'Tis not for nothing the good bellyful,
> The warm serge, and the cord that goes all round,
> And daylong blessed idleness besides.

It was for this reason that Augustine so strenuously insisted on the necessity for manual labour. 'Servants of God,' he wrote to Bishop Aurelius and his monks, 'soldiers of Christ, know you not the plots of the treacherous foe who has scattered everywhere so many hypocrites under the guise of monks, who traverse the provinces without mission, without home, never fixing their abode anywhere? Some of them carry the relics of martyrs, or what they pretend to be such, and know how to make use of them; others boast of their amulets and prophylactics; others, not shirking from the guilt of lies, declare that they have relations and kinsmen in such and such a country, and are on their way to visit them. All of them insist and demand that money should be given them, either to meet the wants of their lucrative poverty or to reward their pretended virtue.' Thus the pretence of saintly mendicancy became the reality of greedy imposture. Monasticism thus early filled the land with sturdy adventurers, and—as Bonaventura says of the Minorites—men shunned a begging friar who was seen on a road at a distance, as if he were a pestilence.

Augustine seems also to have been the founder of the first nunnery in Africa. There had always been virgins who had consecrated their life to God, but they do not seem to have been collected into one community in these dioceses until he gathered a number of them together at Hippo under the rule of his sister, a pious widow who numbered the daughters of Navigius among her nuns. Augustine could rarely be induced to see them, and never alone, or unless the need for his presence was urgent. He once had to write a severe letter to a body of nuns who were clamouring for the deposition of an abbess whom they disliked; and he seized the opportunity to sketch out for them a prescribed rule.

Even during the five years of his presbyterate Augustine rendered great services to the church, in which he was assisted by Aurelius, the able Bishop of Carthage. From the first he was engaged in those struggles against heretics and schismatics, of which we shall speak farther on. In 393 he was invited by the bishops assembled at a council of the African church to preach before them 'On Faith and the Creed', and afterwards to publish his address.

So great was his reputation that Valerius was in constant dread of his being seized and nominated for some bishopric, and on one occasion he was only able to avert the danger by hiding him in a seclusion where no one could find him.

Augustine began his correspondence with Jerome and with Paulinus of Nola, for whom he had the highest admiration and esteem. By exerting the full force of his will and eloquence he put an end to one of the very worst customs of the church. Chiefly through his appeal to Aurelius, a canon had been passed by the Council of Hippo which forbade bishops and presbyters to banquet in the churches, but it was not so easy to restrain the licence of the people. There was a festival of some saint annually observed at

Hippo, which was known to the people by the name
Laetitia, 'joy', and on this day Catholics and Donatists alike
abandoned themselves to the wild excesses of gluttony and
drunkenness. Augustine was told that the people would
not tolerate the prohibition of their annual revel, and took
the occasion afforded him by the gospel for the Sunday to
denounce the custom in a sermon on 'Give not that which
is holy to the dogs'. The sermon was widely discussed and
severely criticised, and he returned to the same topic in a
powerful Lenten discourse on driving out those that
bought and sold in the Temple. He entreated the congregation with tears not to drive him to extremes, and when
he had moved them also to tears he hoped that he had carried his point. But when the morning of the festival
dawned he was told that some of his people were still
determined to hold their *Laetitia*, and since he knew not
what more he could do he determined to enter the church
to preach to them on Ezekiel 33:9—'But if you do warn the
wicked man to turn from his ways and he does not do so,
he will die for his sin, but you will be saved yourself.'

If they still persisted, he determined to shake out his
garment against them, and depart. Happily, before noon,
the people came to a better mind; and abandoning his prepared discourse Augustine preached an extempore sermon, in which he told them that their bad custom had only
arisen from a concession made in earlier days to idolaters
who missed their heathen feasts. He entreated them
henceforth to rise to higher things, and to imitate the
other churches in which there never had been this bad custom, or in which it had been voluntarily abandoned. He
carried the people with him. The hours which would have
been degraded by sensual excesses were spent in psalmody
and worship.

Another bad custom which the eloquence of Augustine
abolished was the *Caterva*—'a small but serious and bloody
encounter which took place yearly at Caesarea in
Mauretania, in which the inhabitants of the city were

divided into two armed bands, fathers against sons, or brothers against brothers, and fought to the death for five or six days, until the town flowed with blood. No imperial edict had availed to uproot the hateful custom. . . . Augustine harangued the people against it, and was deafened with their applause, but continued to speak to them till their tears flowed.' From that time the custom disappeared.

Among the books which he wrote during this period were those *On the Usefulness of Believing; On Two Souls; On Lying*, which was partly aimed at Jerome's view about the dispute at Antioch; and commentaries on the Sermon on the Mount, and the Epistles to the Romans and Galatians. He also wrote many of his letters.

8

Bishop

In the forty-fifth year of his age Augustine was consecrated coadjutor-bishop of Hippo. Valerius, who was now
feeling the burden of age, had long desired to secure him
as his successor, and thought that the surest method would
be to have him appointed his coadjutor. Awaiting the
opportunity of a visitation of Megalius, the Metropolitan
of Numidia, he secretly invited Aurelius of Carthage to be
present at the same time, and then in a sermon before the
assembled bishops and clergy he published the design
which had hitherto been kept a profound secret. It was
welcomed by the people with a shout of joy.

But there were two difficulties to be removed. Augustine
himself had never heard of coadjutor-bishops, and he
would not consent to be consecrated until it had been
proved to him that there had been many instances of such
elections both in Africa and in other churches. Neither he
nor Valerius knew that the appointment of coadjutors,
except in very special circumstances, was forbidden by the
eighth canon of the Council of Nice. Afterwards, when he
was made aware of this canon, he would never allow it to
be broken, and to prevent such mistakes hereafter he procured the passing of an order that henceforth the decrees
of the canons should always be read to priests and bishops
before they were ordained.

The other difficulty was more formidable and more painful. The primate, Megalius, had a strong prejudice against Augustine, and refused to consecrate him, making against him some serious accusation, of which the nature is not mentioned. Augustine treated the charge with absolute disdain, and when Megalius in a council of bishops was ordered to produce his proofs he completely broke down, gave to Augustine his written exoneration from the calumny, and begged the pardon of the council for the fault which he had committed. He consecrated Augustine, who freely forgave him; but there seems to have been some continuing unpleasantness in the relations between them, for when Megalius died shortly afterwards, Augustine wrote to his friend Profuturus, Bishop of Cirta, in somewhat mysterious terms, 'Scandals are not lacking, but there is also a refuge; sorrows are not lacking, but there are also consolations.'

Now that Augustine was a bishop he felt himself bound by the duty of hospitality, and could no longer be a monk; but he lived in a clergy-house surrounded by his presbyters and deacons, and made no change in the simplicity of his habits. He would ordain no presbyter at Hippo who would not conform to his rule, and he degraded those who abandoned it. He had conquered the temptations of his youth, and could say to God with all his heart, 'Thou biddest me to be continent; give me what thou biddest, and bid what thou wilt.'

He watched with almost morbid scrupulosity against any excess in eating or fondness for particular kinds of food. He drank wine, and though he was never drunk he was never quite satisfied that he did not take more than was absolutely required. He watched with great jealousy over the least delight either in sweet odours or sweet sounds, and so morbid was his scrupulosity that he was almost inclined to condemn any fondness for church music as a sin, unless his pleasure in it was derived exclusively from the words and not from the melody. He not only guarded himself from every form of sinful passion, but scrutinised the working of all his senses, and if he sometimes felt curiosity in watching a dog chasing a hare, or lizards or spiders catching flies, he reproved himself if he did not immediately connect the incident with some religious meditation. The one temptation which he now felt it most difficult to overcome was the love of human praise.

In his dress he avoided alike the affectation of poverty and the ostentation of display. His undergarments were of linen, his outer garments of wool, and over all he sometimes wore a sort of coat worn also by laymen, and called *byrrhus*. If anyone gave him a garment it was regarded as common property; if it was splendid he sold it and gave the proceeds to the poor, regarding it as unbecoming to a bishop of humble origin to wear rich attire. He never wore a ring on his fingers. He could not fulfil what he strangely regarded as the gospel rule of wearing no shoes. His health was too weak for this; he was intensely sensitive to cold, and he regarded the rule as not obligatory, because he found from the gospel that Christ himself wore shoes.

The ordinary food of his table consisted of vegetables, though meat was furnished to guests or to the weak. None of his clergy might drink more than a certain number of cups of wine, one of which was forfeited if they fell into the bad habit of swearing. The spoons were of silver, the rest of the table furniture was of earthenware, wood, or marble. He kept open house for guests known and unknown, and it was one most admirable rule of his hospitality that all calumny, slander, gossip, and spite were absolutely forbidden. On the table was an inscription—

Let him who takes pleasure in mauling the lives of the absent know that his own is not such as to fit him to sit at this table.

Nor did the inscription express a mere idle sentiment. On one occasion some of his fellow-bishops showed themselves unmindful of it, and Augustine severely reproved them, saying that either the verses must be obliterated from his table, or that at any rate he would leave them in the middle of his meal and retire to his chamber.

He was unable to find time for the manual labour which was wisely required in most monastic bodies. The care of the church, with the studies and labours which it involved, made incessant demands upon him, and he found little leisure even to read. He grew old before his time in consequence of ill health, which made it sometimes necessary for him to retire into the country for brief periods of rest and refreshment.

The expenses of his clergy-house were paid out of the revenues of the church, of which the remainder was given to the poor. He made it an absolute rule that his clergy were to be a communistic body living in the bishop's house, and none of them calling anything his own. If anyone reserved anything for himself, he did so secretly and in violation of a distinct understanding. He would not accept a presbyter on any other terms. If one of his clergy did reserve property, he was not allowed to assign it to anyone by will, and his name was struck off the list of Augustine's clergy. 'Let him invoke a thousand councils against me,' he said, 'let him sail where he likes to denounce me, let him lie anywhere he can, God will help me that he shall not be a cleric where I am a bishop.' In all this he went beyond his mark, and set up an arbitrary tyranny not in accordance with scripture precedents; nor did the plan work well, in spite of his perfect sincerity.

He set a noble example in the matter of legacies, which he refused to accept when he thought that they were unfair to the family of the testator. He admired Aurelius because, having received a legacy from a man of wealth who had no children, he at once restored it when a child was unexpectedly born to him. He refused the heirdom of an estate from a father who, in a fit of anger, had disinherited his son. He refused a legacy from Bonifacius because it involved the charge of shipping and the peril of sailors. Once, after he had received a deed of gift for a large property, the giver changed his mind, asked that the legal documents be restored to him, and offered a hundred pounds to the poor instead. Augustine at once abandoned his legal rights, restored the deeds, and contemptuously refused to receive the money from such a donor. He advised Alypius to behave in the same way in the matter of a disputed possession at Thiava, since it was always his principle to avoid giving grounds for criticism.

There were many who murmured at his magnanimity, because they desired to see their church enriched, but it was infinitely better to be scrupulous in such matters than to show the rapacity for which the clergy of that day were so notorious that laws of mortmain had to be passed against them.

He resisted the passion for building because he thought that it involved worldly anxieties, but he encouraged his presbyter Leporius to build a hospice with money contributed for the purpose. He had a poor-box in his church, and depended on the voluntary offerings of his people to supply him with money sufficient to meet the needs of the poor. He constantly impressed on them the duty of charity and almsgiving, which he sometimes exercised to save debtors from imprisonment. When other means were lacking he did not hesitate to follow the noble example of Ambrose in melting the church plate to find funds for relieving paupers or prisoners.

Like other great bishops of the day, he often flung the mantle of the church over the miserable and oppressed, though his appeals to the civil authority on their behalf were always modest and respectful. The best bishops of the church were also the ablest, wisest, and most disinterested of the defenders of the people.

As a preacher he took great pains with his sermons. They are never grand orations or elaborate theological treatises or pieces of ornate rhetoric, like those of the great Cappadocian Fathers. They were meant for the rude fishermen of Hippo, not for the polished reasoners of

Antioch or Constantinople. They were short, plain, evangelical, and influenced by circumstances. He regarded it as the utmost triumph of Christian oratory to promote edification, and he thought that this could best be obtained by directness and simplicity, not by exhaustive treatment and artistic elaboration. He thought carefully over his topic when he could, but he usually trusted for his language to the inspiration of the moment. He was much discontented with his own sermons, and yet he was unanimously regarded as the foremost preacher in the church of Africa.

One secret of his success was that he tried to make himself intelligible to all. His desire was to touch the heart. There is little that is new and original in his discourses, for he aimed at the popularisation of the truths which he taught more scientifically in his formal writings. Even when he preached on such lofty doctrines as the Trinity, he did not dwell upon nice theological distinctions, but treated them as subjects for moral improvement. He gives us his sensibility without his scholasticism. Whether he was dealing with moral ideals or ecclesiastical dogmas, it was his constant desire to promote the life in God.

He felt that the practical instruction which may be derived from sermons constituted one grand and beautiful distinction between paganism and Christianity. Pagan priests sacrificed, but were silent. How could they preach a morality which was so flagrantly at discord with the legends of their own deities? For social amelioration their functions were useless, whereas the Christan bishop or presbyter was the teacher and ennobler of the people, their tribune in peril, their supporter in distress. His sermons were the constant delight of the faithful whom he addressed.

He yielded to what he believed to be divine guidance in breaking off into digressions suggested to him by the moment. On one occasion he asked Possidius and other friends whether they had noticed that he had started a question in his sermon without bringing it to any solution, and had digressed into an argument against the errors of the

Manichees. They replied that they had observed the fact and been astonished by a method which was unusual with him; and he said that he had yielded to a secret impulse. A day or two after there came into the monastery a man named Firmus, who flung himself at Augustine's feet and begged with tears that he would pray for him. He had been, he said, a Manichee, and had given a great deal of money to their 'elect', but had been led to see his error by a sermon of Augustine's. On enquiry they found that the sermon which had effected his conversion was the very digression to which Augustine had alluded. Shortly afterwards Firmus became a presbyter of the Catholic church.

In old age Augustine's sermons became shorter, less rhetorical, and more dialectic. He sometimes omitted a sermon so that the people might meditate on what he had last said. He was anxious not to weary them, and all the more because it was the custom in the African church for the preacher to sit and for all the congregation to remain standing. He felt encouraged by the loud applause of his listeners, but still more when he saw them weeping.

He preached in Latin, and it is a curious fact that he found difficulty in procuring for his diocese a sufficient number of presbyters who knew Latin, and not only Punic. He dealt very plainly with the heresy, drunkenness, and swearing which were the commonest faults among Christians in that day.

His private ministrations were incessant, and all kinds of cases were constantly brought under his cognisance with which he dealt in letters or interviews. One may suffice by way of specimen, as it throws a curious light on the customs of the times. There was a Christian lady named Ecdicia, married to a Christian husband, and the mother of one son. She seems to have been an impulsive person, and in defiance of the injunction of St Paul, she suddenly announced, without the consent of her husband, that she intended, though married, to keep a vow of absolute continence. Her husband, instead of being angry, bound himself by the same vow, and the two lived together in holiness and chastity for many years.

Having thus taken her own course in one matter, she determined to take it also in others. Though ordered by her husband to wear the ordinary dress of a married woman, she chose instead to assume the black garb of a widow or nun. Not content with even this, she disregarded the interests of her young son, and seized the opportunity of her husband's absence to give away nearly all his property to two foreign monks who had received her hospitality, and of whom nobody knew anything. It was shrewdly suspected that the two strangers were not monks at all, but only impostors in monks' garb; and even Augustine assumes that they must have been very dubious characters to accept so much money from an unknown married woman in the absence of her husband.

Maddened by this extravagant folly, the husband broke his vow of continence and plunged into a dissolute career. Under these circumstances Ecdicia wrote to entreat the advice of Augustine. He reproved her severely but justly for her senseless wilfulness, and advised her to win her husband back by humility and prayer, and—if she succeeded—to promise that she would obey him in all things.

Augustine had learnt from Ambrose his exalted conception of the episcopal office and authority, though from the gentler tendency of his character he did not exercise it with so lordly an autocracy. We must, however, remember that in those days the power of a bishop, wielded by a man who was brave and spiritually-minded, was in most instances purely beneficent. It was the necessary counterpoise to a despotic imperialism wielded by officers who were often unscrupulous and practically irresponsible. The dangerous and illegitimate character of the rights which bishops began more and more to usurp is not seen in the lives of men like Basil, Ambrose, and Augustine, but in the arbitrary and intriguing violence of persons like George, Theophilus, and Cyril of Alexandria.

The magnificent pictures of medieval art must not lead us to imagine these prelates moving about in golden copes and mitred stateliness. The mitre was not used till the eighth century. In the fourth, the ordinary dress of the Christian minister was in no way distinguishable from that of laymen, whether pagans or Christians, except by its humility and poverty. We read of splendid vestments which, at this period, began to be bestowed on churches, but Augustine, at any rate, thought it unbecoming to wear them. He desired to be regarded as poor and a teacher of the poor.

9

Controversies with Manicheans

It would prove intolerably wearisome were I to follow Augustine into the labyrinthine theological intricacies of his many controversies in which he discussed and defined almost every outline of the faith. Unhappily for himself, his energies were largely absorbed by polemical discussions; and unhappily for the Western church, his often wavering and subjective decisions were accepted for centuries as the very oracles of orthodoxy.

After his consecration as a bishop, and when on the death of Valerius in 396 he became sole Bishop of Hippo, there is little that is interesting in the development of his character. His biography, diversified by few outside interests, dwindles into a record of his struggles against various heretics. These debates were forced upon him by the events of his day, and by what he regarded as his episcopal duty. By temperament he was peaceful and contemplative, but in the course of year-long discussions he became a hard dogmatist, and his final victory was sometimes won at the cost of love and tolerance. His personality becomes less attractive as his episcopacy becomes more triumphant, until at last the man who sighed so ardently for Christian charity, and was so much opposed to sacerdotal tyranny, uses expressions and arguments which became the boasted watchwords of the most ruthless inquisitors, and are quoted to sanction deeds so unchristian and so infamous as the brutalities of Alva and the massacre of St Bartholomew.

It might have been expected that the still numerous pagans of Africa would have demanded his most strenuous missionary exertions; but his controversies with them were of a far more conciliatory character than those with Christians who differed from the church on points of doctrine or organisation. The paganism of the multitude was often the indignant protest of a nationality which had been crushed by Roman conquests, and barbarous rites still lingered among the Punic population. On the other hand, the paganism of the cultivated classes was as elevated and philosophical as that of Julian himself. Madaura, near his native Tagaste, and the scene of his schooldays, was devoted to paganism, and his friend, the grammarian Maximus, wrote him a remarkable letter from that place, asking him to say who was the God of the Christians, and, setting aside his customary dialectics by which anything could be proved, to give plain reasons why men were to give up the ancient gods for obscure martyrs with uncouth names—Jupiter for Mygdon, Minerva for Sanaes, and all the immortals for the arch-martyr Namphanion or Lucitas. All this reminds Maximus of the battle of Actium, in which the monstrous divinities of Egypt vainly opposed the gods of Rome. The letter is interesting as one more proof how greatly the progress of Christianity was hindered in the minds of cultivated pagans—men like Julian, Eunapius, Libanius, Symmachus, and others—by the gross abuses of relic-worship and martyr-worship. Julian habitually called the Christians worshippers of the dead and of dead men's bones.

Augustine, of course, answered that the worship was addressed to God, not to the martyrs; but that was a feeble defence of a folly which was opposed to the genius of true Christianity. In all other respects he easily answered the letter of the courteous pagan. Why should he ridicule the name Namphanion? Is he so little of an African as not to

know that it means in Punic 'a messenger of good news'?
Were there no base and ridiculous deities in Greek and
Roman mythology? If Maximus has nothing better than
this to offer, Augustine has no time for jests.

The pagans were not converted, but they liked and
respected Augustine; and when the people of Madaura
wrote a letter of introduction to him they addressed it 'To
our father Augustine, eternal safety in the Lord'. It was
only a form, but in his reply Augustine calls them his
'friends and kinsmen'.

The pagan priest Longinian tried also to set before him
the mythic and philosophic view of heathendom as consistent with the purest and loftiest morality, and Augustine's
reply is full of particulars. When the people of Suffecta
had massacred sixty Christians in revenge for the overthrow of a statue of Hercules, Augustine wrote them a
very stern letter; but when the people of Calama, at a
heathen festival, attacked the church, killed several Christians, and endangered the Bishop Possidius, both Augustine and Possidius were more than content with the
punishment of the actual murderers, and did their best to
protect the city from the severity of the imperial
vengeance.

When an African named Publicola wrote to ask Augustine how to act in certain cases of conscience—whether a
Christian might enter pagan ruins, or drink from a stream
the water of which was used in sacrifice, or accept goods
guaranteed by a heathen oath, Augustine answers him
with a calm good sense learnt from the epistles of St Paul.
The Christians of that day were of a generation enfeebled
by long despotism and torn by sects and schisms, but in
Augustine they had a champion of the most splendid
abilities.

But his chief arguments were directed against dissen-
tient Christians. Besides a number of minor struggles
against Tertullianists, Priscillianists, Abelonians, Marcionists, Origenists, Arians, and others, he was entangled

for years in multitudinous debates with the Manichees, the Donatists, and the Pelagians.

The three controversies were widely different in character. The Manichean controversy touched on the very foundations of religious and philosophical belief; the Donatist controversy dealt with issues which were purely ecclesiastical; the Pelagian controversy turned on questions of abstract dogma and speculative theology.

Each discussion left its influence on his own character. Strong as was his opposition to the Manichees, his long participation in their heresy had left deep though unconscious traces on his opinions, and reconciled him to those gloomy conceptions of the future destiny of the majority of mankind which would otherwise have been surely abhorrent to a mind naturally Christian. The struggle with the Donatists launched him into narrow, untenable, and pernicious views of the church, of catholicity, of the relations between civil and spiritual authority, and of the right to control men's consciences by the force of the secular arm—views which were frightfully prolific of curses in later ages. The Pelagian controversy turned on metaphysical and insoluble questions of

Reason and foreknowledge, will and fate,
Fixed fate, free will, foreknowledge absolute,

in which men, like Milton's evil spirits, 'find no end, in wandering mazes lost'. He learnt to identify his own views on these subjects with the infallible verities of the Christian faith; and he furnished the excuse for such fruitless discussions as those between the Jesuits and the Jansenists, and the basis for such dogmas as those of Calvin, with his 'horrible decree'.

Into this complication of strifes we shall not follow him, but shall compress into the briefest possible space the narrative of their incidents.

The first and most continuous of his controversies was with the followers of Manes, whose errors he felt it his special duty to oppose, because for nine years he had been their adherent, and had misled many others into their communion.

Mani, Manes, or Manichaeus, was a Persian who lived towards the close of the third century, but whose biography has become more or less legendary. The odd story of Socrates is that a Saracen named Scythian married an Egyptian woman in Upper Thebes, and there, in various books, introduced the doctrines of Empedocles and Pythagoras into Christianity. He had a pupil named Buddas or Terbinthus, who went to Babylon, added Persian and other Eastern elements to the system, declared that he was born of a virgin, and was finally hurled down a precipice by a devil, leaving his books and a slave boy named Cubricus in the hands of the woman with whom he lodged. The woman enfranchised the slave boy, who, having read the books of Buddas, travelled in Persia, took the name of Manes, and added fresh elements of folly to the system.

He meant to be a reformer of Zoroastrianism, and adopted the central belief of the Zendavesta. He believed in the existence of an Ormuzd (Ahura-Mazda) and an Ahriman (Angro-Mainyas), a good and an evil deity, a principle of light and a principle of darkness, which he identified respectively with spirit and matter. There can be no doubt that he consciously incorporated Christian elements into his system, and also that he shows Buddhist influences in the doctrines of purification by metempsychosis and by gnosis, in the organisation of his followers, and in certain pantheistic views and practices. He was persecuted both by the Christians and the Magians, and was finally flayed alive, by the order of Bariam, about the year 275.

Amid all the uncertainties and confusions, we may perhaps assume that Mani started from Parsism and tried to fuse it with ascetic Christianity, but that he afterwards, in his travels, became acquainted with Buddhism, and that the finer teachings of that religion led him to merge his dualism into a sort of pantheistic monism. 'From one of the grottos consecrated to Buddhism he issued forth with those symbolic pictures which were designed to represent the doctrines revealed to him.'

The original essence of his system was antichristian, for it was dualism, not monotheism. He divided the universe into two kingdoms, the kingdom of light, with its subordinate aeons and angels, and the kingdom of darkness, with its powers of evil. Seeking in vain to fathom the mystery of the origin of evil, he attributed it to the absolute causality of all being. He declared that there were two eternal principles—light, which was good, and matter, which was evil—and that the existing universe was the common product of them both. The impulse to its production came from the restless agitation of the evil principle, and the modes of its creation were set forth in fantastic symbolism. The microcosm of man was analogous to the macrocosm of the universe. In man the spirit or 'the inward man' was the representative of light imprisoned in the evil matter of the body. Concupiscence, the tendency to sensualism, was caused by the triumph of his *material* being; and this was necessitated by the reproduction of his race, so that marriage became of necessity the propagation of sin, since it led to the birth of souls which vainly struggled in the fetters of the flesh.

But though the world represents the partial triumph of evil over good, yet it involves the ultimate triumph of the good over the evil; for the good, though fettered, oppressed, entombed, never ceases to struggle, and thereby to ameliorate and modify the evil, until finally the evil will be reduced to utter impotence. Every flower that blossoms is a triumph of the light; every soul that overcomes sin and seeks after God is a victory of the good. God achieves for the soul what the sun achieves for the flower.

Manicheism was meant to represent the process through which evil was obliterated by the onward and upward progress, the physical and moral elevation of human life. The universe is matter organised with a view to the protection of the divine essence. It concentrates all the means of redemption and deliverance for the captive and imprisoned soul. It does this through the same powers in which the forces of the light have become predominant. These powers are in the material world the sun and moon, the lightships of heaven, storing up all the elements of light uncontaminated by matter; and in the spiritual world, Christ, Mani, and the elect.

The Manicheans freely used the name of Christ, but it was with them the mere adoption of a symbolic phrase. Their Christ was not the Christ of the Gospels. He was to them the spirit of the sun, the light-spirit from the pure light-element of God; not 'true man', but only clothed with a corporeal semblance. Christ on the cross meant to them nothing but an emblem of the sufferings of every soul which strives to become free; and since they held fantastic notions of the joyous and peaceful innocence of the vegetable kingdom, every tree was regarded as a cross on which Jesus hung, and which implicitly contained his body and his blood.

In the system of the Manichees, it had been the main work of Christ to reveal the highest truths whereby men could be set free; but these truths had been speedily forgotten, so that a new and final revelation was necessary. This had been given through Mani, whom they regarded as the Paraclete whom Christ had promised to send into the world.

The 'elect' or 'perfect' were the sacerdotal caste. They were appointed for the perpetual renewal of Mani's influence, by ascetic abstinence from marriage, drink, and animal food. The 'hearers' were those in whom the light-process had only just begun, so that they were intermediate between the mankind of matter and the chosen ones, to whom alone were entrusted the mysteries and the peculiar service of the sect.

The elect were those who, living in celibacy, poverty,

and abstinence, enjoyed to the full the truth, knowledge, and reason which were the watchwords of the Manichees. They boasted of an absolute purity, symbolised by 'the three seals'—of the mouth, which was henceforth to be clean from all evil words, and from all but vegetable food; of the breast, from which all sensuality was excluded; and of the hands, which were to be pure from unrighteous deeds, and from every injury done to the life of nature, since, in their view, every furrow made by the ploughshare, every sweep of the scythe, every plucking of a fruit or flower, was a dreadful wound inflicted on the cross of light which was expanded throughout all nature.

Pure souls set free by knowledge from the curse of evil matter passed first to the sun, then to the starry heavens, finally into the primeval light. Unpurified and undelivered souls had to work out their purification by endless transmigrations, in which they passed through the bodies of animals and plants. Finally, the world would be burnt up, and resolved into its original elements of light and matter; but the powers of darkness would thenceforth be reduced to impotence, and feeling their powerlessness would struggle no longer with the powers of light, but only with themselves.

In many of these fancies we might have seen nothing but the necessary imperfection of a sincere philosophy, vainly struggling with insoluble questions. But the whole system was irreconcilable with Christianity. The Manichees used their dialectic ability to disparage the Old Testament, and to prove that the original revelation, of which it contained only a few discernible traces, had been incurably falsified by Jewish monotheists. They were radically opposed to the demand for faith, declaring that they themselves were placed by reason in possession of certain knowledge. In the Gospels also they declared that there were multitudes of interpolations and contradictions, especially in the genealogies and in the recorded discourses of Jesus. But all the passages in which St John and St Paul speak of the contrasts between light and darkness, the flesh and the spirit, they claimed in support of their own dualism, of which they believed these parts of the New Testament to contain a primitive revelation. Hence they looked upon themselves as the only true disciples of Christ. But their Christ was only a docetic Christ 'who appeared in the form of man but was not man'. (Faustus, the Manichee, taunts the Christians with banishing reason, blindly believing everything, and being as much afraid to separate true from false as children are of a ghost.)

It was part of the danger and evil of the system that they made the freest use of all the language which Christians attached to them, and there is too much reason to believe that some of the mysterious practices which were concealed from the 'hearers', but were known to 'the elect', were of a peculiarly loathly and abhorrent description. In the Christian festivals they took little interest. Their great day—known as 'the Pulpit'—was the feast of Mani, when they all prostrated themselves before a gorgeously draped seat, ascended by five steps, which perhaps symbolised the five elements.

It will be seen at a glance that such a system, with its keen rationalism, its boast of illumination, its richly imaginative symbols, its flattery of the pride of intellect, its constant appeals to liberty, truth, and wisdom, had a strong fascination for many minds. It cannot be denied that, if we were left without any revelation to guide us, dualism might appear to be—as it did to John Stuart Mill—the most reasonable explanation of the phenomena of a universe in which good and evil, light and darkness, life and death, Gerizim and Ebal, blessing and cursing, divide the life of man. It belongs, in fact, to 'a vast indefinite spiritual and intellectual movement, which makes itself felt more or less in the development of every thinking mind'.

Even Christianity fully recognises the existence and the intensity of evil powers, while it offers us the deliverance from them—take, for instance, such phrases as 'the god of this age' (2 Corinthians 4:4); the Jews sometimes went so far as to speak of Satan as 'the *other* god'—but Christianity refers us to the future life for a solution of that riddle of the universe which our limited intellects are here incapable to solve. It was the boast of the Manichees, who in the fourth century had become a powerful and numerous body, that they alone had grasped the key of this mystery; and it was one main work of Augustine to show that their professed solution, not to mention the absurdity of its scientific assumptions, was mixed up with the most puerile fancies, and involved greater difficulties, contradictions, and absurdities, than those which it vainly attempted to remove. He offered a different solution of the problem, and his solution has been accepted in its main features, though not in every detail, by the whole Christian world.

Manicheism seems to have spread with great rapidity. As far back as 287 Diocletian had published an edict against it as 'a new and unheard-of monster which has come to us from the Persians, a hostile people, and has perpetrated many misdeeds'.

Already, as we have seen, Augustine had written three treatises against the Manichees in 388, during the year of his sojourn in Rome, and a fourth—the unsuccessful attempt to explain Genesis by the allegoric method—at Tagaste. When he became a presbyter, in 392, he felt still more deeply the duty of refuting them. His book *On the Usefulness of Believing* was an endeavour to win back Honoratus, who had followed him into Manicheism, by showing the dignity of that principle of faith which the Manichees despised, and by exposing the absurdity of their opinion that the Old Testament was mainly composed of a mass of interpolations. The weakness of the book consisted in its confusion of 'faith' as a principle with 'the faith' as a compact deposit of doctrines.

His next book, *On the Two Souls*, turns on the questions of dualism and monotheism, and develops the deep conception of evil as being nothing but a negation, and therefore as having its origin in the concupiscence of the will, and not in the causality of God. He treats it as belonging to the impulse, but not to the being of the soul.

A third book, *Against Adimantus*, is an attempt to refute the asserted irreconcilability of the Old and New Testaments by proving their relative agreement. The only true and complete method of doing this, by regarding the Old Testament as a progressive but incomplete and imperfect revelation, was unsuspected by Augustine, who was less strong as an expositor than as a dogmatist. The historic method of viewing revelation, though distinctly intimated in the magnificent opening to the Epistle to the Hebrews, and in other incidental utterances of the greatest apostles, remained undeveloped and only partially understood by the church from the time that the narrower Western theologians succeeded in crushing Theodore of Mopsuestia and the school of Antioch, down to the days of Nicolas of Lyra, who died in 1340. The triumph of Latin theology was the death of rational exegesis.

Augustine did not rely on his pen only. He was incessantly challenging heretics to personal disputations, which were taken down by shorthand writers, and widely distributed. It is not astonishing that Augustine was fond of discussion, or that his opponents were far from eager to accept his challenges. Such debates are in nine cases out of ten idle and useless. Each side claims the victory, and the actual or apparent victory is often declared to be on the side of the sharpest dialectician or the readiest talker, quite apart from the real merits of the case. Augustine, a clear and consistent thinker, a powerful logician, a trained orator, a man of perfect sincerity and serene self-confidence, who spoke amid a crowd of admirers in cities where he had attained an influence, would have been a formidable antagonist even had his cause been as weak as it was strong.

When he became a presbyter of Hippo, the Manichean Fortunatus was so much beloved that many embraced his views, and lived in Hippo to enjoy his teaching. Augustine challenged him to a debate, and he was reluctantly obliged by the pressure of his followers to accept the challenge. The discussion turned on the abstract question 'whether there could be two co-eternal and contrary natures'; and since the Manichees rejected authority, it was to be discussed on the grounds of reason. This was debated for two days in September 392, before a large audience assembled in the Baths of Lossius. Augustine insisted on the argument, already mentioned, which he had learnt from his friend Nebridius. If the Supreme God could be injured by the evil he was not inviolable; if he could not be injured he ought not to have placed souls, which are a part of his substance, in bodies which the Manicheans declared to be essentially evil. Fortunatus was wholly incapable of meeting such an antagonist as Augustine; he was overcome, shamed, and silenced. He left the city in deep mortification; many of his followers came over to the Catholic church, and Manicheism ceased to be formidable in the city of Hippo.

After this Augustine was so much entangled in the Donatist controversy that he took no overt step against the Manichees till after he had become bishop. But in the year 404 he challenged Felix, one of their 'elect', who had perhaps been appointed successor to Fortunatus. As Manicheism was now interdicted by the state, Augustine had Felix completely in his power, and all the more because he was not a man of much education. The Bishop of Hippo said to him plainly, 'You must join the Catholic church, or go,' and Felix had therefore no choice but to maintain his faith during a discussion of two days in the cathedral. Augustine repeated the old argument of Nebridius, and Felix was entirely crushed. Nevertheless the management of the discussion gives the impression of unfairness and want of consideration, and the victory is not one which shows Augustine in his most favourable light.

He wrote several other books on the same subject. His

criticism of the Letter of Mani, known as *The Foundation*, which is chiefly remarkable for the charitable tone towards those in whose belief he once had shared, contains the memorable but not very happy assertion that Augustine would not have believed the gospel had he not been moved thereto by the authority of the church. He here shows himself far less wise than Luther, who placed the church as far below Christ as the creature is below the creator. If the Catholic faith depended so exclusively on external authority, many a Manichee might prefer a faith which he believed to be in accord with his own heaven-bestowed reason—with the spirit of man, which is the candle of the Lord.

The most important of Augustine's anti-Manichean writings is the work *Against Faustus*, in thirty-three books. He wrote it in answer to urgent requests, since everyone regarded Faustus as the leading Manichean teacher of his day, and Augustine's work contained some of the most formidable criticisms of the sect against the lives of the patriarchs and other parts of the Bible. Faustus also made some powerful and thoroughly true remarks, which it would have been well if the church had accepted as a warning against the fatally increasing tendency to set dogma above holiness, orthodoxy above morals.

'I have learnt,' he said, 'to despise silver and gold; I carry no money in my purse; I am content with my daily bread; I take no thought for the morrow; I have no cares about food or clothing; and you ask me whether I accept the gospel. You see a man poor and patient, a man of pure heart, a sufferer, hungry, thirsty, persecuted and hated for righteousness' sake, and you doubt whether I accept the gospel.

'But you say, "To accept the gospel means not only to obey its commandments, but also to believe everything which is written in the gospel, and therewith, first, that God was born." We reply that faith consists of two parts—partly in Word, that is, in knowledge of the Person of Christ; and partly in Works, namely, in keeping the commandments. See then how much loftier and harder a part I have chosen for myself, and how far lower and easier a part you have chosen for yourself. Naturally the multitude streams to you and departs from me, because they know not that the Word of God stands not in word but in power. Why then do you molest me, who have undertaken the difficult part of faith, and left the easier part to you as to the weak?

'But you say, "I hold the part which you have abandoned as the most important and essential for the obtaining of salvation, namely, the knowledge that Christ, God in Christ, was born." Well, then, we will ask Christ himself, and learn to know out of his mouth the condition of our salvation. "Who, O Christ, shall enter into thy kingdom?" He answers, "He who doeth the will of my Father which is in heaven."'

It was an obvious answer that faith in word, faith show-ing itself in the right apprehension of doctrine, was a direct aid to faith in works; nevertheless Faustus, heretic as he was, here expresses nobly and evangelically one essen-tial factor of the truth, and there can be no greater curse to any church than the depreciation of well-doing in com-parison with orthodox doctrine. The worst of heretics is not the incorrect thinker but the bad man. It may be that thousands of those who have been burnt for holding error in things dubious have been far truer Christians than those who have consigned them to the flames. Unhappily the influence of Augustine was a powerful factor in the ten-dency which ultimately set the authority of tradition above the independence of the enlightened reason, and correct-ness of dogma above purity of life.

The little book *On the Nature of the Good* is an enforce-ment of the argument which Augustine regarded as so decisive against the Manichees, namely, the supreme, unchangeable, incorruptible nature of God, and the origin of evil in the freedom of the human will. To overthrow the boasted holiness of the Manichees he tells some terrible stories of their asserted depravity in Paphlagonia and Gaul. It must, however, be borne in mind that Augustine, when he was a Manichee, though he heard of things which seemed to indicate ordinary profligacy, had never seen a trace of the enormities which he denounces.

In the year 405 he wrote his last book against the Manichees, which he also regarded as his best—the answer to Secundinus. Secundinus, a Roman, had written to express profound admiration for Augustine's eloquence, but reprobation for the style of his arguments. He defends the Manichees and disparages the Catholics, roundly charging Augustine with never having understood the real views of the sect which he opposed. 'You are fighting,' he said, 'not against Mani, but against Hannibal or Mithridates.' Augustine, in his answer, takes but little notice of the personalities referred to by Secundinus, but defends the church and refutes the heresy with great force. The spirit of Eastern illuminism differed very widely from that of Christian faith.

The Yezedees or Devil-worshippers of Mosul are believed to be remnants of Manichean sects, and this system left its traces in Muhammadanism.

The chief results of the whole long-continued controversy were the overthrow of the doctrine of dualism; the establishment of the supreme unity of God; the apprehension of evil as an unsubstantial negation; and the tracing of the source of evil to human imperfection. Augustine proves that sin exists neither in God, nor in our own bodily nature, nor in the nature of things which are in themselves indifferent, but in the weakness of our human will. On the questions of election and reprobation, of freedom and foreknowledge, into which the controversy naturally led, Augustine throws no real light. By far the greater part of what has been confidently propounded on these subjects is 'vain wisdom all, and false philosophy'.

10

The Donatists

The deplorable Donatist controversy which troubled the greater part of Augustine's episcopal life was of a wholly different character from that with the Manichees. The questions which it involved were ecclesiastical not metaphysical. They affected church order rather than fundamental belief. They had their origin in furious party spirit rather than in profound speculation.

The schism of the Donatists (so called from Donatus of Cava Nigra, who presided at the Council of Cirta) had now raged for nearly a century. It began in the persecution of Diocletian, who, in the edict of 303, had ordered the Christians to give up their religious books under pain of death. This law was strongly enforced in Africa. Some Christians evaded it; others, among whom were some of the clergy, gave up their Bibles, and were called by the scornful name of *Traditores*. They defended their conduct by passages in the Old Testament, and by the argument that a man's life is more sacred and precious than a written book.

The condemnation of their weakness was all the more severe because at that time the Montanists had filled Africa with the spirit of ferocious zeal. Mensurius, Bishop of Carthage, deceived the pagan commissioners by giving up *heretical* books, while concealing the others; but he and his archdeacon, Caecilian, had given deeper offence by opposing the extravagant honours heaped by Christians, and especially by women, on the imprisoned confessors. Many of these were persons of no real worth, and the motive of some had been mere vanity and a superstitious desire to purchase an easy forgiveness for lifelong delinquency. It was therefore deemed undesirable by the bishop that they should be treated as though they were saints and half-divine. These 'confessors' consequently did their utmost to undermine Mensurius, and they were aided by a wealthy and bigoted widow named Lucilla, whom the bishop had exasperated by reproving her for kissing the bone of a supposed martyr before the Eucharist. 'At that time,' says Optatus of Mileum, one of our chief authorities, 'the anger of a perturbed woman generated the schism, faction nourished it, and avarice confirmed it.'

On the death of Mensurius in 311 Caecilian had been somewhat hastily consecrated bishop by Felix of Aptunga. The Numidian bishops had been absent when he was chosen, and they made common cause against him with Lucilla, and a body of jealous presbyters and church-wardens from whom he had demanded the restitution of certain plate and other church property. They said that he was half a *traditor* himself, and had been consecrated by Felix, whom they charged with the same offence. He offered to refute all the charges brought against him, and said that if they could prove that his consecration was irregular he would come to them and be consecrated again. 'Let him come for imposition of hands,' said Purpurius, a Numidian bishop notorious for his frantic language, 'and we will break his head by way of penance.'

(At the end of the Council of Cirta in 305 the presiding bishop, Secundus, had accused Purpurius of having murdered two nephews. 'I am not to be frightened by such questions,' he replied; 'I have killed and will kill all who stand in my way.' At this strange synod another *traditor* was

appointed Bishop of Cirta. Yet these very bishops joined in
the attack on Caecilian! The Council of Eliberis (Elvira), at
which Hosius was present, and which passed important
canons on church discipline, was held about the same
time.)

No reconciliation was possible with ruffians of this
stamp. They therefore consecrated a favourite of Lucilla,
the reader Majorinus, and, on his death in 315, Donatus,
who excluded Caecilian from the church and headed the
schism with such furious and eccentric ability that it
became known by his name.

In 312, Constantine, by the advice of Hosius of Cordova,
endeavoured to end the schism, and told the Proconsul of
Africa to put it down by force. As the Donatists appealed
that they should not be condemned unheard, he entrusted
the case to Melchiades, Bishop of Rome, who in 313, with
the approval of eighteen other bishops, decided for Caecilian, but did not exclude the Donatists from the communion of the church. The Donatists refused to abide by the
judgement, because nothing had been said about their
chief objection, which was that Felix, the consecrating
bishop, had been a *traditor*. Constantine then directed that
Felix should be tried at Carthage, and the whole dispute
submitted to another council at Arles. Felix was acquitted
at Carthage, and the Donatists were condemned at Arles
(314). As they again appealed to Constantine to hear the
case in person, he consented, though with reluctance, and
having heard Caecilian and Donatus plead their cause
before him at Milan in 316, he once more decided in
favour of Caecilian. But to end the whole quarrel he
imprisoned both of them at Brescia, and sent two bishops
in whom he had confidence to consecrate some new and
undisputed prelate in their place. Meanwhile, however,
Donatus escaped from custody and Caecilian followed
him.

Constantine, thoroughly disgusted, ordered the
Imperial Count Ursacius to suppress the Donatists with

the sword; but he found it impossible to do so. In 321 they wrote to the Emperor that they refused to have anything to do with his 'scoundrelly bishop'.

Donatus must have been more than the mere haughty self-seeker whom his enemies describe. Augustine himself admits his sincerity and influence, and compares his character to that of Cyprian. He won many adherents, and the indignation against secular violence kindled the counter-fanaticism of the wild *Circumcelliones* who embraced his cause and spread terror far and wide in Africa for many years, mingling their frantic follies with the grossest excesses of open sensuality. The cause of the Donatists must not be judged by these lawless and ferocious marauders, though some of the bishops connived at and even utilised their frenzy. But finding that the schism only grew worse, Constantine rushed from the excess of severity to the excess of tolerance, washed his hands of the whole business, and saying that he left it to the judgement of God, actually built for the Catholics, at his own cost, a church to make up for one of which the Donatists had dispossessed them by violence! They grew so rapidly in numbers and influence that at a synod in 330 they had 270 bishops present.

Under such circumstances the Donatists soon filled Africa, though every other church of Christendom acknowledged Caecilian as the true Bishop of Carthage.

Constantine died in 337, and his son Constans tried to smooth matters down by gifts and flattery. He sent two commissaries, Paulus and Macarius, to promote peace; but while Gratian, Bishop of Carthage, hailed them as 'servants of God', a Donatist writer describes them as two wild beasts, who brought with them 'the polluted murmur of persecution'. Donatus rejected the gifts of these commissaries with the words, 'What has the church to do with Caesar?'

The fanaticism increased. The Circumcellions behaved like the anabaptists and Fifth Monarchy Men of the Reformation age, and the civil power was obliged to reassert itself. The chief bishops were expelled, and Donatus died in exile. When Julian became Emperor, in order to promote dissensions among the hated 'Galileans' he allowed all banished bishops to return, and the Donatists came back in triumph, headed by their new bishop, Parmenian. They seized their lost churches, and to purify them from the contamination of Catholic possession, washed their walls and floors, and even dug up and ejected the bodies of the dead.

Gratian renewed the edicts against them in 377, but they grew in numbers until they began to split into 'sub-dichotomies of petty schism'. They soon became a party with nothing left but a nominal principle, which alike in theory and in practice they had repeatedly violated. They began in religious rigorism, and ended in unreasoning fury.

Optatus, Bishop of Mileum, had written seven books on the Donatist schism, but as yet no one had risen to confute their whole theory. This task was undertaken by Augustine after he became Bishop of Hippo, in 396. There was need for his intervention, for at Hippo the Donatists were more numerous than the Catholics. The province was specially afflicted with the fury of the Circumcellions, who claimed the impulse of inspiration for their worst atrocities. The quarrel was so universal that it introduced the most painful divisions into the heart of families. Causes of dispute were constantly arising between the antagonistic communities. At one time Augustine complains that the Donatists had received and rebaptised a brutal and dissolute youth who had murdered his own mother. At another time a subdeacon, a bad character, had been expelled from the church but rebaptised by the Donatists, and had openly joined a villainous band of Circumcellions. At another, Augustine had been assailed with maledictions by a Donatist presbyter, and called a perverter and a *traditor* because, at the request of a father, he tried to persuade a female catechumen to return to the church.

These incidents led to internecine opposition between Christians, united in creed though differing in discipline. But Augustine, swayed by the principle of authority, was especially scandalised by the triumph of disunion. He began to preach against the Donatists, to write against them, and to challenge them to discussions. At first he addressed them in the friendliest way, and repudiated all recourse to violence or state interference. It was only at a later stage that his views deteriorated until he had learnt to oppose party spirit in the fiercest spirit of party, and to invoke the secular arm to rivet the fetters of resisting consciences. It was thus that the courteous reasoner became the oracle of persecuting intolerance.

The Donatist Bishop of Hippo at that time was the aged and blameless Proculeianus. Augustine at once wrote to invite him to a conference. At first he seemed inclined to discuss the questions at issue with only ten witnesses present on each side. But he changed his mind. He returned no answer to a highly respectful letter of Augustine, and suddenly broke off all intercourse with him. Augustine in point of fact never succeeded in obtaining from the Donatists one of those public discussions in which he had been so successful against the Manichees. Once, indeed, at Tubursis, he had a friendly interchange of opinions with Fortunius, the excellent Donatist bishop; but the next day so many persons crowded to hear their conversation and so repeatedly interrupted it by exclamations and arguments that it had to be broken off and was never renewed. He was therefore obliged to have recourse to his pen. But it is doubtful whether any discussion would have removed the misconceptions which arose from fundamental differences of view. The church of which the Donatists were mainly thinking was the ideal invisible church, which depends on the holiness of its members; the church of which Augustine was thinking was the visible church, with the notes of 'catholicity' and apostolic succession.

Parmenian, who succeeded Donatus about 350, had

written a celebrated letter against Tichonius, the author of the *Seven Rules of Exegesis*, which Augustine himself adopted. In this letter he gave the Donatist version of the origin of the schism, and tried to prove from theory and from scripture that it was a duty to separate from the 'apostate' Catholics.

In answer to this letter Augustine wrote in 400 his *Three Books Against the Letter of Parmenian*, in which he gives the Catholic account of the origin of the schism, answers Parmenian's arguments, and turns against him his own scripture proofs. In this book he lays down the rule that though the purity of the church demands the punishment of individual sinners for their own good, yet when the bad are numerous it is impossible and wrong to use extreme measures against them, but the tares must be left to grow with the wheat until the harvest. He also shows that the Donatists had given up their own chief points of contention by admitting without rebaptism some of those who had left them, and by sanctioning the violences of one of their bishops, Optatus, who had received the scornful nickname of the Gildonian Optatus, because of his close alliance with the pagan general Gildo.

Soon afterwards he wrote his *Seven Books on Baptism*, in which he shows against the Donatists that the efficacy of the sacrament is not affected by the unworthiness of the minister, and especially argues against the authority of Cyprian, who had induced a council at Carthage to reject the baptism of heretics.

He was next compelled to answer a letter of Petilian, who had been a lawyer and a Catholic catechumen, but had been won over to the Donatist schism by the offer of the bishopric of Cirta. This man had attacked the church in a contumelious manner, complaining of the injuries inflicted on the Donatists, and calling the Catholics a body of *traditores*. The letter was regarded as a powerful polemic, and Augustine in three books refuted as much of it as he had been able to obtain.

Petilian was so infuriated by arguments which he could not answer that he took refuge in a violent personal attack on Augustine himself. He raked up every rumour and scandal which he could find to his discredit, charging him with crimes which he had never committed, upbraiding him with all that was darkest in his own *Confessions*, saying that he had been a Manichean presbyter, and had in that capacity been guilty of many enormities. He compared him to the orator Tertullus; sneered at his specious dialectics; revived the old calumnies on which Megalius relied when he opposed his consecration; accused him of literary dishonesty; abused him for instituting monasteries; and in general overwhelmed him with a turbid stream of atrocious calumnies.

The attack recoiled on himself. It at once revealed to all but the dullest understandings that to the arguments of Augustine he had no reply to offer. His slanders only proved the baseness of his own mind, and admitted of an easy refutation. Augustine replied to them with the utmost calmness and dignity. He declined to join Petilian in a contest of mutual mud-throwing. 'Were I,' he said, 'to answer your revilings by my revilings, we should then simply be two revilers, and we should inspire the serious with repugnance and the frivolous with malignant delight.' He would not defend himself further than by saying that whereas he repudiated his life previous to his baptism, and did not desire to remember it except to glorify God's mercy, he could appeal to all who knew anything about his subsequent conduct when he said with St Paul, 'My conscience is clear' (1 Corinthians 4:4). Regarding Petilian's attacks on the church, he showed that they proved nothing with respect to the real controversy, and that, so far as they had any truth in them, they told as strongly against the Donatists as against the Catholics.

He continued the controversy in 402 in his book *On the Unity of the Church*, and in his four books in answer to the grammarian Cresconius on baptism and rebaptism.

Unfortunately his arguments produced no appreciable results. The parties faced each other with an antagonism all the more implacable because the ultimate questions at issue between them were secondary and ecclesiastical. Violence became the order of the day. Each side tried to proselytise. The outrages of the Circumcellions were repaid in the same coin, and each party said to the other, as Luther said to Zwingli, 'You have a different spirit from ours.' It seemed as if the glory and usefulness of the church of northern Africa would suffer utter shipwreck on the rock of schism. There were rival bishops—a Donatist and a Catholic—in every large town.

Augustine and other African bishops would have been glad of any reasonable compromise. In 401 a council at Carthage left each bishop to adopt the best means in his power for procuring unity. But patience and charity were lacking. The Catholics tried to set the Donatist congregations against their leaders, and to secure the aid of the civil power. They sowed the wind and they reaped the whirlwind. Such was the fury of the Donatists that the lives of the bishops were endangered. The excesses of the Circumcellions—who, like the anabaptists of the sixteenth century and the Camisards of the eighteenth, arrogated to themselves the exclusive title of saints—would be incredible, if they were not a recurring phenomenon at times of religious excitement. They traversed northern Africa in gangs of idle and plundering rascality, which they disguised under the pretence of religious zeal. Pillage, murder, and conflagration accompanied their footsteps, until their war-cry of 'Praise to God' and the sight of the huge clubs which they called 'Israels' became the terror of the country. They confounded suicide with martyrdom, and often gave to the hapless traveller the choice between murdering them or being himself murdered.

On one occasion Augustine's friend Possidius, Bishop of Calama, was attacked by an armed band led by a presbyter related to the Donatist bishop. He was compelled to take refuge with his friends in a farm, which was immediately surrounded by armed men. After an attempt to set it on fire, the door was burst open, the horses and cattle killed, several people wounded, and Possidius himself dragged down from the upper storey, insulted and beaten. Restitutus, a Donatist presbyter, having gone over to the church, was attacked by Circumcellions headed by their clergy, dragged out of his house, brutally beaten, dressed in a coat of rushes which they called a *buda*, thrust into a muddy pit, and kept for twelve days in the hands of his persecutors. He was thenceforth regarded as a confessor, and afterwards as a martyr.

Another presbyter named Marcus, who had also left the sect, was saved from murder by an opportune rescue. Another converted presbyter named Marcianus only escaped their hands by flight, but their clergy seized his subdeacon and nearly stoned him to death, for which they were punished by having their houses razed to the ground.

The Circumcellions lay in wait for Augustine himself on one of his episcopal visitations. Had they succeeded in their ambush he would probably have been murdered, but by a providential 'accident' the guide of his party missed his way and took the wrong turning at a place where two roads met. Augustine arrived at his destination by a circuitous route, and thus escaped the plot.

Servus-Dei, a bishop of Thubursica, in endeavouring to recover a church from the Donatists, had to fly for his life, and his aged father, who was a presbyter, died of the injuries which he then received.

Maximian, Bishop of Baga, in occupying a church assigned to the Catholics, had to take refuge under the altar from a band of armed Donatists. The altar was broken over him, he was beaten with its fragments, and after much violent treatment was stabbed in the groin with a dagger, and filled the sacred place with blood. He was only prevented from bleeding to death because the dust through which he was dragged coagulated over his wound.

The Catholics, singing psalms, tried to rescue him, but the Donatists tore him from them, and supposing him to be dead, flung his body into a tower, where he lay senseless on a heap of refuse. Here he was found by a peasant, who with his wife removed him to their cottage and nursed him until he was healed of his ghastly wounds, of which the scars remained till the day of his death. He went to Rome to appeal for justice to the Emperor, and it was partly with reference to his case that Honorius passed at Ravenna in 405 the severe penal laws which the terrified Catholics now demanded at his hands. These 'Edicts of Union', as they were called, forbade rebaptism on pain of confiscation of property, gave freedom to any slave whom his master compelled to join the Donatists, and enjoined the civil authorities to enforce a strict observance of these laws.

Under these circumstances, Donatists came over to the church in large numbers, and in 407 another council of Carthage ordained that they should be received in peace; but the stronger-minded remnant, who would not accept fear as a reason for nominal conversion, regarded themselves as the 'little flock', the 'church in the wilderness', and, welcoming every form of martyrdom, were driven into the extreme of party fanaticism.

Both sides show the deadly evil of religious controversy. The Donatists began as rigid evangelicals, they ended as ruthless brigands; the Catholics began as tolerant churchmen, and ended as bitter persecutors. Augustine himself, whose views in 404 had been mild and charitable, had become much less tolerant by 407. In answer to the remonstrances of his former friend Vincentius, who had become the Donatist Bishop of Cartennae, he now first used the evil and perversely sophistic arguments which were destined to be, for so many ages, the watchwords of religious persecution. Nothing, he said, was more compassionate and charitable than to repress and punish heresy by the aid of the civil power, because 'the Lord disciplines those he loves', and because the state was now Christian, and it was, therefore, its present duty to protect the truth and punish its enemies!

In his own diocese the adoption of strong measures was fatally unsuccessful. It was devastated by bands of Circumcellions. They set fire to buildings, they destroyed harvests, they forced people to receive their baptism. Armed with all kinds of horrible weapons, they attacked and ransacked the houses of the orthodox clergy, seized them, beat them, wounded them, and flung them away half dead. With an excess of atrocity they also filled the eyes of many with chalk, and, finding that they recovered from this treatment, they afterwards mixed the chalk with vinegar, and thus blinded them by slow tortures.

'They live as robbers,' complained the clergy of Hippo to the Donatist primate, 'they die as Circumcellions, they are honoured as martyrs, and yet we never heard that even robbers have blinded those whom they plundered.' They blamed their enemies for their own suicides, and did not blame themselves for the murders they committed. Nor were their wrath and despair confined to this diocese. In Baga they burned a church and flung into the fire the sacred books, the preservation of which, in the Diocletian persecutions, was the reason for founding their sect. In Liberalis they destroyed the church. At Cirta they destroyed all the altars. At Caesariana their bishop plundered the property of the church, and at Pudentiana he destroyed four basilicas. At many places there were serious riots which ended in bloodshed.

The triumph of persecuting orthodoxy was short-lived. In 408 Stilicho, the great minister and general of the feeble Honorius, was murdered in consequence of a court intrigue, and, a year after, his successor Olympius was driven from power. Then followed a complete reaction in the court at Ravenna. In 409 the penal laws against the Donatists were repealed, and whole churches of them at once seized the opportunity to abandon their hypocritical conversion. Honorius, in answer to yet another appeal,

summoned a conference to meet in 410, at which Marcellinus, a friend of Augustine, was to hear and to decide the
case as Imperial Commissary. It met in 411, and consisted
of 279 Donatists and 286 orthodox bishops, for whom
Petilian and Augustine were to be the respective spokes-
men.

It was clear that such a conference, 'over which,' as
Athanasius would have scornfully remarked, 'a Count
presided,' could decide nothing. How would Augustine
himself have felt had Marcellinus been an avowed and
notorious Donatist, and a personal friend of Petilian?
Would he, in that case, have preached the opening
sermon, and promised that the orthodox bishops would
resign their sees if the cause was decided against them?
Marcellinus offered that there should be a second presi-
dent. 'We do not want two,' answered Petilian, 'for we
never asked for even one.'

The discussion of the first two days turned on the question which side had first invoked the civil power. On the
third day the real points at stake—the origin of the schism,
and the true purity of the church—came under discussion.
The discussion was perfectly hollow. It was rendered all
the more tiresome because the Donatists said that they
could not possibly sit down before so great a man as Marcellinus, so that he and the bishops had to remain standing
all the first day; and the second day Petilian said that scripture forbade them to sit down by the words, 'I will not sit
with the wicked.' Indeed, the temper shown by the
Donatists throughout was inexcusably bad. When Augustine, on the third day, began his speech with the word
'brethren', Petilian repudiated it as an injury. They
attacked Caecilian's memory, and yet declared that they
would not enter into the history of the schism. Some of
them proposed to interpret the word 'Catholic' to mean
those who kept the laws and observed the sacraments, but
they were compelled into admitting that they did not
believe the whole church to be limited to Africa.

As a matter of course, after eighteen days' conference, Marcellinus decided against the Donatists, and Honorius confirmed his decision by the re-enactment of severe decrees. The Donatists protested that they refused to accept the arbitration of laymen in church questions, and things went on as before. The Donatists answered the appeals of their opponents with bitter and ambiguous words. 'I cannot prefer what you will,' said Emeritus, 'but I can will what I will.'

Augustine began to speak of the orthodox victory in the Conference of Carthage.

'Men can see from the records,' answered Emeritus, 'whether I was defeated or victorious, and whether I was defeated by the truth or suppressed by force.'

'Why, then, did you come here?' asked the Bishop of Hippo.

'To give you this answer, once for all,' replied Emeritus.

Of what use was it to argue against the practical master of so many legions? When the Imperial Tribune threatened Gaudentius of Tamagunda with death unless he came over to the church, 'Know,' he answered, 'that, if you apply force against us, I and my people will go to our church and burn it over our own heads.'

'You had better make your escape,' said the Tribune, 'or you will be put to death.'

'We do not seek martyrdom,' answered Gaudentius, 'but we are quite prepared for it. It is only the hireling who fleeth because he seeth the wolf coming.' Augustine told the Donatists that they could not be Christians because they complained that they had no place to flee unto!

The incident gave rise to the last anti-Donatist writing of Augustine, *Against the Letters of Gaudentius*, which shows evident signs that he had begun to be tired out by the endless controversy. Gaudentius had deplored that, in consequence of the severity put into force against them, thousands of Donatists had been driven into a perfect frenzy of suicide. Augustine replies that more had come over to the church than had committed suicide. The Catholics held it better that 'a few abandoned and desperate men should perish than that a vast number should be left to burn in Gehenna for belonging to a deadly schism! The church would console herself by the peace she had acquired through severity, as David consoled himself for the death of Absalom.'

The incursion of the Vandals effected that termination of the schism which neither the lenity nor the persecution of the church had been able to achieve. Sterner and sterner laws to suppress Donatism were passed by Honorius, and an inextinguishable and indomitable remnant still defied them. But, in 420, the Arian Vandals burst into Africa, and persecuted Donatists and orthodox alike. The opponents were united by common and frightful peril, and then first discovered that, accepting the same creed, believing in a common Saviour, it ought not to have been so insuperably difficult for them to combine. The last sparks of the schism were stamped out by the Saracens in the seventh century in the universal ruin which destroyed the church of northern Africa.

Augustine had to face for many years the hatred of this party, because he exhausted every ecclesiastical, literary, and political method to secure their overthrow. The controversy brought into prominence a new set of questions as to the idea of the church, and the relations between church and state, which had only been partially stirred by the Montanist, Novatian, and Meletian schisms. The only doctrinal question incidentally involved was that of baptism. Augustine himself admitted that the Donatists were not heretics, although he regarded their schism as being no less culpable than heresy. The tedious and heated discussion had a bad effect alike on his temper and his theology. It made him severe where he had once been gentle, and narrow where once he had expressed larger views.

It had been the sincere desire of the early Donatists to keep the church pure, and it was their sincere belief that no church could be the true church which was not so. Their first movement had shown a stern reaction against indifferentism, worldliness, and the slumber of discipline in the now victorious church. Such a reaction was neither unnatural nor unworthy when we remember that all the great Fathers in succession admit that the hour of the church's political triumph had also been the commencement of her spiritual deterioration. Nevertheless, the Donatists were in the wrong. Their belief that the unworthiness of ministers destroyed the efficacy of the sacraments led to cruel and monstrous conclusions. Their view was too haughtily zealous and pharisaic. It might almost be said to them, as Constantine said to Acesius, that 'they had better get a ladder and try to go to heaven by themselves'. They were separatists who had no objective proof of their pretensions to be the sole true church, and whose subjective claims fell to the ground because they could only be tested by that knowledge of the heart which is in the power of none but God. If only a church absolutely pure could claim to be the true church, there could be no true church at all. The brutalities of their Circumcellions, the violences of their Gildonian bishop Optatus, the dissoluteness, drunkenness, and suicide of many of their adherents, were sufficient to prove the impossibility of their ideal. Alike in their appeals to the state and their admission without rebaptism of their own sectaries, they had again and again abandoned the very principles on which they had been founded.

Having proved all this with unanswerable force in various writings, Augustine proceeded also to show that the orthodox church was the true church. Its objective existence centred not in the righteousness of all its members, but in Christ and his righteousness. If its ideal had been destroyed because there had been found a few *traditores* among its clergy, how yet more fundamentally must the claim of the Donatists have been destroyed by the abominations of the Circumcellions!

So far so good, but Augustine fatally injured a good cause when he adopted, without explanation and limitation, the hard, false, pharisaic assertion that only churchmen could be saved. He had neither the right nor the warrant to confine by human and invented limitations the freedom of the Holy Spirit of God. And this error led him to others. He hazarded the assertion that for schismatics and heretics Christ's death was of no avail, and that their faith, their sacraments, even their sincere self-sacrifices and martyrdom, were perfectly valueless. He came to regard the Christian presbyterate as endowed with a sort of ideal, impersonal holiness, and supernaturally sacerdotal power. He fell into the fatal error of thrusting the church between the soul and God, and thrusting the clerical caste between the laity and the church.

The exaggeration of the authority of bishops had begun with the letters of Ignatius, of which the interpolations show to what blasphemous lengths their folly had advanced. Cyprian had followed in this unfortunate direction. Sharing with most of the Fathers a complete unacquaintance with the progressive character of revelation, devoid of any true conception of the relation of the Old Testament to the New, he transferred to Christian ministers all the Mosaic notions which apply exclusively to hereditary priests. He applied the story of Korah to show that all heresies arise 'from not obeying the priest of God', who is 'a judge in the stead of Christ'.

Tertullian had at least learnt from Montanism a clear view of the universal and unconfined workings of the Spirit, and said, 'It is (only) the authority of the church which has established a difference between the ordained and the multitude.' But Cyprian had in this respect entirely forgotten the lessons of his master, and Cyprian, not Augustine, must be regarded as the main founder of that dangerous tyranny which succeeded for so many centuries in robbing the laity of their divine, inherent, indefeasible rights as a royal and universal priesthood. The church which has begun to identify 'the church' with the clergy is on the high road to perversion of all that is most essential in gospel truth.

While rightly rejecting the Donatist assertion of a divine authorisation by dreams, miracles, and the hearing of prayers offered at the graves of martyrs, he shows no real ground for claiming every passage which speaks of the church in scripture as though it applied to his own exclusively. His dialectics here become arbitrary and biassed, and possess no argumentative force. Nor are his objective marks of the church much more decisive.

The Donatists claimed the note of catholicity because they defined catholicity to mean that the church possesses universal truth; Augustine made it consist objectively in universal diffusion and continuous existence, and subjectively in the episcopate and in charity. He distinguishes between the ideal and the visible church, because the latter is as a herd in which there are both sheep and goats, and a net in which there are both good and bad fish. He wavers in his interpretation of the rock on which Christ built his church. In some passages he explains it of Peter himself, and in others of Peter's confession. He seems to have held finally that Peter was meant, but only ideally as a representative of a true knowledge and confession of Jesus as the Christ.

But Augustine's system breaks down because he wanted his church to be catholic and yet exclusive, universal and yet Roman. He confuses, as men have done ever since, an ideal and a concrete, a real and a purely empiric, catholicity. He was unable to recognise that the church is not one *fold*, nor was it ever promised or ever desirable that it should be gathered in one earthly fold; but that it is, always has been, and to the end of time ever will be, one flock of many folds (John 10:16).

It required a long experience of history to show that the main function of the church is to meet and satisfy the varying religious needs of varying men in different ages; that unity is quite compatible with wide diversity; that different forms of organisation and service are a divine necessity to prevent torpor and universal paralysis of independent thought; and that difference of spiritual attitude must be met by diversities of gifts and of administration. It took centuries for men to discover that 'the church of God is a congregation of faithful men wherein the pure word of God is preached, and the sacraments are duly administered in all things necessary to the same'; that there never has existed, and never can exist, one branch of the church which can claim the exclusive title of catholic; and that the catholic church is that which is known to God only, and is not confined within the narrow pales of any single community. *Except* when the word 'church' is made coextensive with all true seekers after God and all true children of God, whatever be the communion to which they belong, the assertion that men can only be saved 'in the church' is an arrogant and cruel falsehood. Yet it has led men to believe such inconceivable absurdities as that a true church cannot exist without episcopacy, or that no Protestant, or no Roman Catholic, or no Nonconformist, can possibly be saved!

In that part of the controversy which touched on baptism Augustine may be regarded as entirely in the right. The whole Christian church of the East and West has agreed that when it has been administered in its simple essentials it ought never to be administered again.

But there was another most important element of the controversy in which the theory of the Donatists, whatever may have been the inconsistencies of their practice, was right; and in which the Catholics, headed by Augustine, in his later, harder, more dogmatic, and episcopal spirit, were absolutely and with fatal consequences, though perhaps inevitably, in the wrong. The church had no right to invoke the power of the state to persecute those who differed from itself. Heretics and orthodox in turn fell into this evil habit. In endeavouring to crush the independent prerogatives of the human conscience, they were often guilty of quenching the light of the Spirit and storming the very citadel of heaven.

Augustine must bear the fatal charge of being the first, as well as one of the ablest defenders of the frightful cause of persecution and intolerance. He was the first to misuse the words of the parable, 'Compel them to come in'—a fragmentary phrase wholly unsuited to bear the weight of horror for which it was made responsible. He was the first and ablest asserter of the principle which led to Albigensian crusades, Spanish armadas, Netherlands' butcheries, St Bartholomew massacres, the accursed infamies of the Inquisition, the vile espionage, the hideous fires of Seville and Smithfield, the racks, the gibbets, the thumbscrews, the subterranean torture-chambers used by churchly torturers who assumed 'the garb and language of priests with the trade and temper of executioners', to sicken, crush, and horrify the revolted conscience of mankind. The spirit of paganism was not intolerant. Libanius and Julina knew that fire and sword may make martyrs and may make hypocrites, but cannot change a man's real faith. It is mainly because of his later intolerance that the influence of Augustine falls like a dark shadow across the centuries. It is thus that an Arnold of Cîteaux, a Torquemada, a Sprenger, an Alva, a Philip the Second, a Mary Tudor, a Charles IX and a Louis XIV can look up to him as an authoriser of their enormities, and quote his sentences to defend some of the vilest crimes which have ever caused men to look with horror on the religion of Christ and the church of God.

And his view was a fatal retrogression. There was no excuse for it except the involuntary and unconscious deterioration caused by the spirit of episcopal domination and priestly self-assertion. The old view of the church had distinctly been, 'Violence is hostile to God.' The early Christians, in the days when they themselves were weak and persecuted, had always argued against the right to use force in questions of religion. This had been the view of Origen and of Athanasius. 'Nothing,' says Athanasius, 'more forcibly marks the weakness of a bad cause than persecution.'

When Ambrose and Martin of Tours indignantly exclaimed against shedding the blood of heretics, and refused to communicate with those who had ordered the execution of the heretic Priscillianists, they were only continuing the early traditions of the church.

'It belongs,' said Tertullian, 'to the human right and natural power of each man to worship what he thinks right, and the religion of one is no advantage or injury to another.'

Gregory of Nazianzus had always expressed his abhorrence of persecution, his determination to employ no methods but those of moral persuasion.

Even under Constantine, Lactantius had written that 'Religion cannot be enforced; we must act with words rather than with blows, that the will may be with us. Nothing is so voluntary as religion.' And again: 'We do not demand that anyone should against his will worship our God, who is the God of all whether they will or no; nor are we angry if they worship him not.' And again: 'Religion is alone the seat in which Liberty has placed her home. It is a thing which, beyond all things else, is voluntary, nor can necessity be imposed on anyone to worship what he does not wish. A man may perhaps pretend, he cannot will to do it.'

Augustine himself in his earlier days had repeatedly argued that the true method of dealing with heretics was by reasoning and forbearance. How fierce would have been the indignation of the Christians if Julian had passed an edict inflicting capital punishment on all who practised the rites of Christianity! And yet Augustine asks the Donatists: 'Which of us, which of you, does not praise the imperial laws against the sacrifices of pagans? . . . The penalty for that impiety was death.'

The appeal to the arm of the law was suicidal, for it might at any time be turned against the orthodox, and then they would have had no right to complain. The church was perfectly justified in appealing to the state for the protection of itself against Circumcellion marauders; she had a perfect right to claim that robbers and murderers should be punished and executed; but she had no right whatever to claim the suppression of Donatists as Donatists, or Manichees as Manichees. To treat the church as superior to the state, and yet to use the state as a subordinate in doing its own unpleasant work, was a degradation to church and to state alike. The excellent Bishop Optatus of Milevis had written far more truly: 'The state is not in the church, but the church is in the state.'

Is anyone so Erastian as to be able to read without a smile of indignation the decree of Theodosius, Gratian, and Valentinian II, in which 'a rude Spanish soldier and two feeble boys' command the world in general to believe whatever is believed by Damasus, Bishop of Rome, and Peter, Bishop of Alexandria? The Donatist bishop Gaudentius wisely said: 'God appointed prophets and fishermen, not princes and soldiers, to spread the faith.' Augustine's best efforts could adduce no tittle of New Testament argument in favour of that irreligious persecution, which could only be purchased at the cost of religious independence. All he could offer was the overstrained and wholly irrelevant fragment of a parable, 'Compel them to come in.' That scrap of text and shred of metaphor, by the help of the supposition that by 'the highways and hedges' were meant schisms and heresies, was made to bear the intolerable weight of guilt caused by the self-assertion, egotism, and opinionativeness of religious hatred! Of course Augustine had ready some arguments (such as they were) which he inferred from scripture; for

In religion
What damned error but some sober brow

> Will bless it and approve it with a text,
> Hiding the grossness with fair ornament?

But they were almost exclusively derived from those Old Testament passages which, in the total absence of the historic conception of scripture as containing the fragmentary records of a partial and progressive revelation, have been adduced to sanction almost every form of human crime.

They were more worthy of such a writer as Julius Firmicus Maternus than of the Bishop of Hippo. In his sanction of religious intolerance, in his appeal to persecution, Augustine fell behind the ablest of his contemporaries. Nay, in this matter Augustine might have learnt wisdom from the pagan sophist Themistius, who held that God left man's soul free to judge of religious truths; and even from the apostate Julian, who thought that 'neither fire nor sword could change the fate of mankind', that 'the heart disowns the hand which is compelled by terror to sacrifice, and that persecution only makes hypocrites and martyrs'. History had already shown with sufficient clearness that religious cruelty always provokes reprisals. Julian's one mistake in forbidding the Christians to teach Greek literature had been appealed to as an excuse for the edicts of Theodosius against the pagans.

The invaders of the rights of conscience hypocritically professed to preserve the freedom of conscience, on the plea that they only removed obstacles from the progress of truth. Cruelty was made to bear the semblance of mercy by professing to be undertaken in the eternal interests of the persecuted!

'Outside the church is no salvation'—that was the first assertion, which was hopelessly falsified by the second, 'There is no church but mine'; and this was made a deadly proposition by the conclusion: 'It is therefore in your own interest (as well as mine!) that I should force you into (at least nominal) membership of the church by tyrannising over your will and conscience; by making you accept my convictions as your convictions, whether you hold them or no; and by reducing you into pauperism, driving you into exile, or putting you to death, if you refuse.' Man has no immunity from erroneous opinions, and therefore it is not for man to arrogate to himself the infallibility of God or to anticipate his judgements.

The following earlier declarations of tolerance may be noted:

Tertullian: 'God has not hangmen for priests. Christ teaches us to bear wrong, not to avenge it.'

Athanasius: 'Satan, because there is no truth in him, breaks in with axe and sword. But the saviour is gentle, and forces no one to whom he comes, but knocks and speaks to the soul, "Open to me, my sister."'

So too Hilary complains that the church, once herself exiled and imprisoned, is now using the terrorism of exile and prison.

Chrysostom: 'Christians are not to destroy error by force and violence, but should work the salvation of men by persuasion, instruction, and love.'

Has it ever been worthwhile for 'the church' to sprinkle her white robes with the blood of the innocent, and arm her gentle hand with the hellish implements of torture, in order to secure either a dead level of torpid ignorance, or an empty assent, a hypocritical uniformity, a perjured and soul-destroying profession of beliefs, which the free conscience is led by God's Spirit to reject? The blood of the martyrs whom 'the church' has slain cries against her from the ground to God and man. The Donatists had more truth on their side when they quoted the words of Christ, 'No-one can come to me unless the Father has enabled him' (John 6:65). They argued that 'if Christ had loved his opponents in the same fashion that churchmen did, he would never have died for them', and that he had set an example to his followers, not how to slay their enemies, but how to suffer in their stead.

And when Augustine boasted that violence had succeeded,

that many of the Donatists had been converted (strange conversion!) by the persecuting edicts of Honorius, he strangely deceived himself. He had made a wilderness, and he called it peace. To such a man it should have been no excuse that he was goaded into oppression by the obstinacy and crime of the party opposed to him; still less should he have been driven into extremes by his own logic, radically vitiated by a false conception of the idea of the church. The history of the north African church, even as we learn it from his own pages, shows that persecution produces nothing but the sham conversion of some and the intensely maddened fanaticism of others. Party terrorism never produced sincere conversion. Prudentius admits that the penal edicts of Theodosius against paganism had practically failed.

Augustine had as little right to glory in the Donatists who were frightened into nominal uniformity as pagans had to boast of the apostates and renegades who gave up books or burnt incense in the Decian and Diocletian persecutions.

The state has no power over religious belief. Caesar may enforce obedience to Caesar's laws; but to reckon heresy or schism among evil actions is to assume an infallibility which, as has been proved by numberless experiences, does not belong to any state or to any religious community. When Caesar seized the sword to enforce the gospel, Augustine ought to have been the first to say to him, in the words of Christ, 'Put your sword away!' (John 18:11).

If the orthodox party had insisted on the civil suppression of all crimes against property and person; if they had firmly put down the Circumcellions, while at the same time they behaved to their brother-Christians with tolerance and charity, provoking them only to love and good works; if they had striven only with fair, strong, and kindly argument, urged in the spirit of Christian forbearance, either the Donatist schism would have ceased to exist or its existence would have been a dwindling and a harmless one. As it was, these unfortunate schismatics became a source of peril and destruction. Reduced to despair by persecution, the unhappy rigorists sided first with the Vandals, and then with the Arabs. Being oppressed, they found their deliverers in the barbarians.

'These events,' says Niebuhr, 'should be a lesson to those who are determined not to see the misfortune which is the result of intolerance, or, as it deserves to be called, injustice.'

We conclude then that the Augustine who, in 397, assured the excellent Donatist bishop Fortunius at Tubursicium that he entirely disapproved of persecution, was a far wiser, if not a better, man than the Augustine who, in his later years, degraded the plea of mercy as an excuse for deeds of persecution, and became the purveyor of 'nests of sophisms' to all who sought to secure religious peace by violence, and religious unity by sword and flame. But on this question we may appeal from the later to the earlier Augustine, who wisely wrote in his commentary on St John's Gospel,

> If we are *dragged* to Christ, we believe against our will; violence therefore is applied, the will is not kindled. A man may enter the church against his will; he may receive the sacrament against his will: believe he cannot except with his will. If we believe with the body, we might believe against our will; but we do not believe with the body. Hear the apostle: '*with the heart* man believeth unto justification'. . . . Since he who is dragged seems to be compelled against his will, how do we solve the question 'No one comes to me unless my Father enables him'?

Unhappily, the church took a downward course for many centuries in the matter of religious persecution. A century later persecution was in the ascendant, and later ages had learnt to witness it with impotent horror or ferocious joy.

11

The Pelagian Controversy

The East had been convulsed by questions about the Godhead; the West was now to be agitated by a question about manhood. As the dogmatic definition of the Trinity and the twofold nature of Christ had been chiefly elaborated amid the theological struggles of Eastern councils, so now it was to be mainly left to the Fathers of the West to lay down the doctrinal limits of questions which bore on sin and grace.

The Manichean controversy turned on philosophical speculations; the Donatist on matters of church order; the Pelagian on questions of religious dogma. As Cunningham puts it: 'The dispute with the Manicheans centred in the *metaphysical* question as to the nature of evil in the universe. . . . The dispute with Pelagius was chiefly concerned with the *psychological* question as to the nature of evil in the heart of man.'

In all three controversies Augustine was actuated by a noble zeal, and rendered to the church many memorable services. Yet those services were by no means unmixed with evil. The environment of controversy which led Augustine, as it led Jerome, to suspect heresy from afar, had a deleterious effect alike on his temper and on his theology. It cannot be said that he 'improvised his convictions', but he was sometimes dragged into exaggerations of them by the sophistic plausibility of his own remorseless logic.

The Manichean controversy was the first which led him into the habit of attaching deeper importance to theoretic orthodoxy than to personal religion, and even those who revere him see the evil effect which it continued to exercise on his whole teaching.

The Donatist controversy launched him into intolerant conceptions of church authority and dangerous misuse of the powers of the state.

The Pelagian controversy ended in his producing a system of scholastic theology which tried to define the indefinable, introduced into Catholic doctrine a complete novelty, and was prolific of horrible inferences dishonouring to God and revolting to the conscience of mankind. Happily his rigid theories seem to have exercised but little influence on his habitual teaching. In all his 400 sermons, and I know not how many homilies, the theory of reprobation is practically non-existent. He felt the danger of preaching predestination, and he always addresses his hearers as beloved of God, and designed for salvation.

Pelagius, or Morgan, perhaps a monk of Bangor, was the son of poor parents, who early left his home and travelled southwards. He was a man of natural but self-taught genius. Of the personal details of his life we know but little. After a short stay at Rome he went to Constantinople, where he enjoyed the warm friendship and esteem of Chrysostom. He there became acquainted with the theology of Origen and of the Greek Fathers, which coincided with the natural bent of his own generous heart. When Chrysostom fell a victim to the infamous intrigues of the clergy, women and eunuchs of his bad metropolitan city, Pelagius returned to Rome and was confirmed in his life of stern asceticism by what he saw of the corruption to which Jerome also bears witness as prevailing even among the clergy of the Western capital.

In Rome he wrote the only works of his which have

come down to us—a commentary on the epistles of St Paul, a letter to the virgin Demetrius, and a profession of faith addressed to Innocent the First. No one at Rome saw any heresy in his commentaries.

Like Jerome, he enjoyed the friendship of many illustrious families, and trained many young persons in the paths of the ascetic life. Against the perfect innocence and purity of his conduct not even his enemies had a word of proof. (Jerome and Orosius, indeed, charge him with luxury, but Pelagius had lived in friendship with Paulinus of Nola and other saintly persons, and Augustine speaks of him personally with respect.) We may be sure that he was a thoroughly good man, for though Augustine and Jerome anathematised him as a heresiarch, Augustine calls him 'a pre-eminent Christian', and his personal excellence is admitted even by so unscrupulous a controversialist as Jerome.

Perhaps the Pelagian controversy would never have arisen at all if the views of Pelagius had not been pushed into extremes by his friend and follower Coelestius, whom Jerome, in his usual fashion, described as 'stodged with Scotch porridge'. Pelagius, a man of calm temper, broad sympathies, and peaceful conscience, a clear thinker and an excellent exegete, had not the least sympathy with the prevalent delight in religious disputes. His heresy was in him hardly a heresy at all, for he approached it only on the practical side, and never pushed his dubious premises into inferential extremes. He saw that many excused their vices on the plea of human weakness; and this seemed to him a dangerous error. Had it not been for Coelestius on one side and Augustine on the other, Pelagius, in spite of mistaken views, of which he certainly had no monopoly, might have died in the odour of sanctity and been regarded as one of the Fathers of the Church. The errors in his extant writings are certainly not worse, and are far less dangerous, than those which might be culled from the pages of many a writer whom nevertheless the church has honoured.

But Coelestius was a man of a more restless and aggressive character. He carried his old instincts as an advocate into his new position as a monk and theologian. In 411, after a stay at Rome, in which they had won general approval, the two friends travelled to Sicily and Africa. They passed through Hippo, but failed to see Augustine, who was engaged in crushing the Donatists at Carthage, where Pelagius met him once or twice, and they exchanged friendly letters. Pelagius travelled to Palestine. Coelestius unfortunately became a presbyter at Carthage. At first the pure life and many gifts of Coelestius secured him much favour, but the next year Paulinus of Milan, the biographer of Ambrose, warned the Bishop Aurelius that he was teaching error, and quoted from his writings seven distinct or inferential propositions which he declared to be heretical; as—

1. That Adam would have died even if he had not sinned.
2. His fall affected himself alone.
3. New-born children are in the same position as Adam.
4. Mankind neither dies through Adam's death nor is raised by Christ's resurrection.
5. Children, even if they die unbaptised, have eternal life.
6. The law, as well as the gospel, can lead to holiness.
7. Even before Christ came there were men without sin.

On 'original sin' Coelestius had nothing to say. He regarded it as a mere scholastic enquiry, depending for solution on the open question between *creationists*, who thought that each soul was a fresh creation, and *traducianists*, who thought that souls were derived *ex traduce* from the parents. As for infant baptism, Coelestius said that he regarded it as a duty, though he hardly explained why. A council was summoned, and leaving other questions on one side they anathematised the seven propositions, and expelled Coelestius, who went to Ephesus, and there continued his work as a presbyter.

Augustine, though absent from this council, approved its decisions, and shortly afterwards, at the request of

Marcellinus, explained the doctrine of original sin in his three books *On the Punishment and Forgiveness of Sins*, and further in a book *On the Spirit and the Letter*. It is note-worthy that Augustine held a view which has been ignor-antly regarded in modern times as heretical, namely, that *not all punishment beyond the grave is necessarily endless*. After saying that some believed in 'temporary punishments' only in this life, and others in the period between death and the final judgement, he implies an intermediate state, and a sort of purgatory. Yet he says nothing of man's incapability of good, and makes allowance for the freedom of man as well as for the grace of God. Both of these Pelagius always professed to recognise, though he seems to have confined 'grace' to the influence of the ordinary means of grace, and certainly did not go so far as to regard it as 'a sort of fourth person of the blessed Trinity'. Unfortunately the one Latin word *gratia* was used to render the two Greek words *charis*, 'favour', and *charisma*, 'a spiritual gift', and this led to some confusion; but Pelagius used 'grace' in a very vague and subordinate way, and he had as little conception of that absolute spiritual union with Christ on which St Paul so greatly dwells as he had of the race as dying in Adam. But if Pelagius almost did away with grace, Augustine, in spite of his assertions, almost did away with free-will.

Meanwhile Pelagius in Palestine had enjoyed friendly relations both with Jerome and John of Jerusalem, though he was much more closely drawn to John than to the nar-row and jealous theology of Jerome. Jerome at once began to discover the real or imaginary taint of Origenism in the opinions of Pelagius. A noble young Roman lady named Demetrias had taken the vows of a nun, and Pelagius as well as Augustine wrote, at the request of her mother, to congratulate her.

This letter stirred up the whole controversy. Pelagius began it with a eulogy on the loftiness of human nature, and an argument against extravagant assertions of 'total corruption of the will'. There had been, he said, virtuous men before the Advent, and since then it had been easier to live a holy life. Men and women could live holy lives in any condition, so that virginity, though honourable, was not to be overvalued. Much of this was true and wise, and Pelagius showed a higher wisdom than either Jerome or Augustine when, though himself an ascetic, he refused to be swept away by the current opinions on the subject of celibacy, and resisted the Manichean error by which those opinions were deeply though unconsciously affected.

In 415 there came to Palestine a young and fiery Spanish presbyter named Paulus Orosius, the author of the well-known history, an uncompromising champion of orthodoxy and a zealous admirer of Augustine. He was scandalised that a man against whom Augustine had written should be living in high repute at Jerusalem, and still more by the disdainful question of Pelagius, 'And what is Augustine to me?' He attacked Pelagius before a synod of the assembled clergy of Jerusalem, but further discussion was at the time impossible. Bishop John could not understand Latin and Orosius could not understand Greek, and, with the exception of an untrustworthy interpreter, Pelagius alone was familiar with both languages. Since, however, the question had first been raised in the Latin church, it was left to the examination of Innocent at Rome.

Eager, however, to secure a condemnation of these opinions in the East as well as in Africa, the opponents of Pelagius induced Eulogius of Caesarea, the Metropolitan of Palestine, to summon a synod, at which two Gallic bishops, Heros of Arles and Lazarus of Aix, were to accuse Pelagius of heresy. The synod of fourteen bishops met at Diospolis (Lydda) in 415, but neither Orosius nor the two Western bishops appeared. Pelagius refused to be held responsible for anything which was not in his own writings; he maintained that in asserting the possibility he had never asserted the *reality* of a sinless life; that in arguing for the free-will of man he never excluded the grace of God; and that he was in entire accordance with all the

recognised doctrines of the Catholic church. He declined
to answer for the opinions of Coelestius; declared that he
did not hold the views attributed to that presbyter; and on
being asked to anathematise the holders of certain errors,
said that he was perfectly willing to do so if he might anathematise them not as heretics, but as fools. The bishops
were satisfied and Pelagius was acquitted. Unfortunately
many admirers of Pelagius vented their indignation at the
splenetic sarcasms of Jerome against the 'miserable synod'
by a most unjustifiable attack upon the monastery at
Bethlehem. This did not improve his already embittered
feelings towards 'Catiline', as he chose to nickname the
new heresiarch.

Orosius hurried back to Augustine, who once more
seized his pen to maintain the total depravity of human
nature in his works *On Nature, On Nature and Grace*, and *On
the Perfection of Human Righteousness*. In these works he is as
extreme on his own side as Coelestius, if not Pelagius, had
been on the other. Two new councils were summoned to
condemn Pelagius at Carthage and Mileum, and the acts of
these councils, together with a confidential letter from
Augustine and his friends, were sent to Pope Innocent.
Pelagius also wrote to Innocent, asserting that he had never
denied the necessity of grace or the duty of infant baptism.
He sent a confession of his faith and charged his opponents
with Manichean and Jovinian errors, since their doctrines
implied that some men could not possibly help sinning, and
others, being predestined to eternal life, could not really
sin at all. Innocent, delighted that he should be appealed
to, promptly used his apostolic infallibility to excommuni-
cate Pelagius, Coelestius, and all their followers.

Augustine, on receiving the Acts of the Synod of Diospolis, wrote his books *On the Dealings with Pelagius*, and a
letter to Paulinus of Nola, which is of extreme importance,
as containing the first formulation of the theory of predestination, into which he had been gradually dragged by
the course of the controversy, and which he founded

almost exclusively on incidental expressions in the Epistle to the Romans. Pelagius wrote once more to defend what he really held, and to repudiate what he did not hold. Coelestius hastened to Rome, where Innocent had been succeeded by Zosimus. Zosimus, who, being a Greek, had but little taste for these questions, accepted the favourable view of their opinions, and held with them that 'original sin' was not a recognised doctrine of the church, and that other points at issue were mere school problems. Looking at the question simply on its practical side, he wrote to reprove the African bishops for their excessive zeal in heresy-hunting, for their uncharitable haste in condemnation, and for the vain curiosity of systematising refinement, which led them to be wise above what is written. He said that the Romans could scarcely refrain from weeping at the condemnation of men who spoke so often of the 'grace of God', and the 'divine assistance'. He finally told them to submit to the authority of the see of Rome. This they were quite ready to do when the Pope agreed with them, but when he differed from them it was an altogether different matter. Failing with the Pope, they secured the Emperor, and having found from the Donatist controversy how effective is the syllogism of violence, they at once obtained from Honorius at Ravenna a *sacrum rescriptum,* which banished Pelagius and Coelestius out of the empire, and threatened their followers with confiscation and exile. This was probably effected by Augustine's influence with Count Valerian, and it was said that in order to secure this interference of the secular power to control theological opinions, bribery was freely used.

Another African council of 200 bishops, in 418, anathematised the views of Pelagius. Thereupon Zosimus, in sudden alarm, turned completely round, and declared strongly against Pelagius. Eighteen bishops of Italy, and with them the able and excellent Julian of Eclanum, refused to accept the new decision, and were driven into exile. All Pelagians, and all who supported them, were punished, and Pelagianism as an external heresy was effectually crushed. Of Pelagius and Coelestius we know no more; they died in obscurity and neglect. Julian alone maintained the controversy, in which the happiness of his life was shipwrecked. He was powerless to withstand the twofold force of the imperial authority and the passions of the mob to which Augustine had equally appealed, and to which the trimming Pope had instantly yielded.

'Why,' he indignantly asks Augustine, 'did you hire the populace, and stir up factions at Rome? Why, out of the revenues of the poor, did you fatten troops of horses through almost all Africa? Why, with the legacies of matrons, did you corrupt the powers of the world, that the straw of popular fury might blaze against us? Why did you scatter the peace of the church? Why did you befleck the age of a religious Emperor with the impiousness of persecution?' To these invectives there was no satisfactory reply, but the arguments of the pious and brilliant Bishop of Eclanum were so keen and strong that Augustine was obliged in 421 to write a careful answer to them in six books.

To this Julian again replied, and Augustine had to consider his refutation so carefully that it remained unfinished even at his death. Julian argued that if every nature was hopelessly tainted with original sin, marriage became a crime; that if there be no real free-will there can be no real responsibility, and therefore no sin and no virtue; that the condemnation of a whole innocent race to total corruption for the sin of one parent was contradictory to reason, to scripture, and to the mercy of God, since it was said in Deuteronomy that each man should suffer for his own sins and not for those of his parents; that if expressions of an opposite import were insisted on, there was no heresy which could not be maintained by scraps of scripture, and that higher than scripture stood a pure conception of the righteousness of God. What would God be if, without either justice or mercy, he punished those whom he had created for evil, and because he had himself created them of the race of Adam? With these and many such considerations he confronted the pessimism of Augustine, which he perhaps rightly regarded as the result of indelible impressions received by the Bishop of Hippo in his Manichean youth—a charge which he vainly attempts to deny. But it was useless to argue. Driven from Cilicia, driven from Constantinople, Julian died at last at the age of fifty, in the deepest poverty and distress, a noble victim to theological intolerance.

Augustine poured forth book after book against the Pelagians, and grew harder and harder both in his expressions and his views as time went on. His anti-Pelagian treatises fill 1400 folio columns of the 16th volume in the Benedictine edition of his works. 'His was the error,' says Canon Mozley, 'of those who follow without due consideration the strong first impression which the human mind entertains that there must be some definite truth to be arrived at on the question. If revelation as a whole does not speak explicitly, revelation does not intend to do so; and to impose a definite truth upon it when it designedly stops short of one is as real an error of interpretation as to deny a truth which it expresses.'

In his earlier books, up to 415, Augustine had forborne to mention Pelagius by name, and spoke respectfully both of him and of Coelestius; but, later on, the Pelagians became 'liars, empty wind-bags filled with their own pride and self-righteousness, not belonging to the church at all, and scarcely worth a refutation'. To all the unanswerable appeals against holding ignoble views of God's character he has nothing to reply but the exclamation, 'How unsearchable are thy judgements, and thy ways past finding out!' He argues that divine grace is not given to all men, which he attempts to prove by the fact that many children die unbaptised! He says that the text, '[God] wants all men to be saved' (1 Timothy 2:4), *must* be misunderstood, since there are so many men who remain unsaved, not because they refuse to be saved, '*but because God wills not that they should*'. He tries to twist '*all men*' into '*men of all kinds*'.

And after all, though he was engaged in this controversy from 411 to the end of his life, he only won a partial victory. In the church Pelagianism vanished, but Augustinianism did not prevail. The church in general rejects the dogmatic Manichean assertion that mankind is split by an iron necessity into two hard antagonistic masses, and that all except a few elect are predestined to endless torments. The monks of Adrumetum thought that Augustine's views would promote on the one side secure indifference, and on the other antinomian desperation.

Cassian, the great master of Western monasticism, disapproved of the exaggeration and one-sidedness of Augustine in one direction, and of Coelestius in the other, and Augustine wrote his *On the Gift of Perseverance* in 425, to combat this Semi-Pelagianism which refuses to accept the 'horrible decrees' of a scholastic philosophy. In this book he sees the harshness and difficulty of his own views, but says that he cannot help this, because they are the word of God. Happily the divinely-implanted instincts and inwardly-illuminated reason of 'the natural man' sometimes help to correct and soften the ruthless interference of 'the unnatural theologian'.

When we consider the excellence of Pelagius as a commentator, and his holiness as a man, we may freely acknowledge that in questions as yet undecided he unduly pressed the power of free-will, and made too little allowance for constraining grace, and yet may be permitted to think that harsh measure has been dealt to him when he is regarded solely as a pestilent heresiarch. His own explanations of what he meant, and modifications of what he said, were scornfully rejected, as well as his repeated declarations that he had always been, and always desired to be, in the orthodox communion of the Catholic church. Had there been less of fervid heresy-hunting, less of passionate misrepresentation, more of lenient construction and Christian charity, he might have survived the misfortune of conflicting with the Western theologians, after having been trained in the larger views of the East. This much at least is certain: he was perfectly sincere.

Both Pelagius and Augustine appealed to scripture, and if they brought to scripture opinions already made, yet each could refer to passages which lent apparent sanction to his own views. Augustine had been convinced of the final truth of his theory by the Epistle to the Romans, and especially by Romans 5 and 9. When he argued in favour of irresistible grace, and absolute predestination, and arbitrary election, he could not but come into sophistic collision with such passages as '[God] wants all men to be saved and to come to a knowledge of the truth' (1 Timothy 2:4), and 'If we deliberately keep on sinning after we have received the knowledge of the truth, no sacrifice for sins is left, but only a fearful expectation of judgement and of raging fire that will consume the enemies of God' (Hebrews 10:26–27). If he had studied St Paul in the original Greek, 'it is probable,' says Bishop Wordsworth, 'that his opinions on predestination, election, and reprobation would have been different from what they were'.

Pelagius could, on the other hand, claim that the reasonings of St Paul could not be so interpreted as to overthrow much that seemed to him to be contained both explicitly and implicitly in the simple teaching of the synoptic Gospels.

Again, both of them appealed to the authority of previous church writers, and here also they might equally claim as many sentences and expressions on the one side as on the other. In point of fact, the truth lay midway between them both, and the earlier Fathers, if they had not been Pelagians, certainly also had not been Augustinians. There were sentences on grace and sentences on free-will in their writings, which, taken alone, might be quoted in favour of either controversialist.

Nay, more, Pelagius, if he vehemently opposed the notion of helpless passivity implied by Augustine's famous phrase in the *Confessions*, 'Give me what thou biddest, and bid what thou wilt,' was yet able to quote from the earlier writings of Augustine himself many expressions which, apart from the plausibility of those ingenious glosses which can make anything mean anything, were in exact accordance with his own views. Unquestionably, Augustine before 379 was himself a Semi-Pelagian. If we take his own words in their plain and obvious sense, he had changed his standpoint; and a writer so progressive and so prolific had need of many reconsiderations of his published views, which attributed sin to the inherent evil of matter. In arguing against the Manichees, he had insisted strongly on free-will as the origin of sin. It was only when the Pelagians saw too exclusively in free-will the source of good as well as of evil that he insisted too exclusively on the irresistible will of God. And he then ran into the peril of degrading free-will into an impotent wicked tendency wholly dependent on a grace predetermined by eternal election.

And whatever may have been the rashness and unwisdom of Coelestius, he maintained with truth that his errors, if errors they were, only affected matters of opinion—matters on which no church had as yet delivered a formal decision, so that even if he were mistaken he could not be heretical. The Greek church has always leaned to Semi-Pelagian views, and was indifferent to the entire controversy. Pelagianism was indeed condemned in the Council of Ephesus, 431, but in the East the question was little discussed, though Theodore of Mopsuestia in 419 wrote against the views of Jerome. 'The English church,' says Dr Neale, 'has from its earliest infancy evinced a tendency to Pelagianism.'

And surely the world has learnt by this time that while there is in this matter no practical difficulty—that while to all intents and purposes man is practically free to refuse the evil and to choose the good, since the grace of God by which this can be done is always and freely accorded to all alike—yet in the theory of the question there lies an insoluble antinomy; it ends, like every other question, in mystery which transcends the feeble capacities of man to understand.

The two disputants were wholly unlike each other. Pelagius, whether he was or not (as some said) physically exempt from sensual temptation, was a man of northern temperament, a severe logician, a clear, calm, consequent, unimaginative thinker, who had lived from childhood upwards the peaceful life of a monk and an ascetic. Augustine, on the other hand, had lived in thunderstorms; he had been a sensualist, a doubter, a Manichee, a rhetorician, an Academic, a man in whose veins ran the hot blood of Africa, and whose whole life had been spent in wild struggles against himself and against his enemies. The hamartiology of Pelagius could hardly fail to misunderstand the hamartiology formed in the burning fiery furnace of Augustine's temptations. There was enough, then, in the dispositions and past experience of the two men to account for wide divergencies in their conceptions of life and of all its moral and spiritual problems; but beside this they approached the questions from wholly different points of view—Pelagius from the side of morals and practice, Augustine from the side of dialectics and of philosophical speculation.

And the extremes of both were dangerous. Pelagianism might make a man unspiritual; Augustinianism might produce a fanatic and a fatalist. Augustine fearlessly rushed forward, or was driven by his antagonists, sometimes changing his opinions as he advanced. Partly from the reasonings of a new religious philosophy, partly by general inferences from limited phrases in the sacred writings, he framed a complete, and, as far as its own consistency went, a harmonious system. But it was the inevitable tendency of this system to give an overpowering importance to 'problems on which Christianity, wisely measuring, it would seem, the capacity of the human mind, had declined to utter any final or authoritative decree'.

He insisted on the acceptance of dictatorial axioms on some of the most mysterious problems which can cross the horizon of human thought, and did his best to identify Christian orthodoxy with inferential logic and vague speculation.

Yet there is one feature of his writings which redounds absolutely to his credit. Dialectical, severe, peremptory, dogmatic as his tone is, he scarcely ever sinks, as Jerome so often does, and as religious partisans do so frequently, into the abusive rancour of personal hostility.

12

Closing Events

It was necessary to dwell at some length on these three great controversies, because they occupied almost all the years of Augustine's episcopal life. Yet such was his comparable versatility, energy, and diligence, that, among the many books which he poured forth on these subjects, he still had time to produce other works of more enduring greatness, while he neither neglected his wide correspondence nor his multitudinous duties as a bishop and pastor of his special flock. He was at one and the same moment the greatest preacher, the greatest writer, the greatest theologian, the greatest bishop, and the most commanding personality in the churches of the West, while he was constantly preaching simple sermons and performing simple duties among the poor artisans and fishermen of Hippo.

His personal life was chequered, like that of all men, with joys and sorrows. Men of a nature like his are always deeply beloved and intensely hated. But if he had many bitter opponents among Manichees, Donatists, and Pelagians—if books full of violent invective were published against him by Petilianus and Julian—on the other hand he enjoyed the passionate admiration of men like Orosius; the warm, unvarying friendship of beautiful souls like Alypius; Evodius, Bishop of Uzala; his future biographer Possidius, Bishop of Calama; Severus, Bishop of Mileum, 'his second soul', 'his other I'. With Paulinus of Nola, whom he never saw, he maintained a delightful correspondence, and his fine spirit of humility and gentleness calmed the tumultuous jealousy of Jerome, and turned a possible enemy into an appreciative friend.

With the Bishops of Rome, except Zosimus, he was in kindly relations, and though he had a theoretic respect for the decision of the see of St Peter, he maintained as strongly as Cyprian and as Hincmar the independence of national churches. In 419 he induced an African council to protest against the pride as well as the unwarranted interferences of the Bishop of Rome.

We have seen already that terrible troubles arose even in the little circle of his monks and clergy. The duplicity of his presbyter Januarius, who practically retained his property while professing to have abandoned it, caused him a severe pang. The unworthiness of the youthful Antonius, whom he had trained from boyhood and recommended for the bishopric of Fussala, almost induced him to emphasise his regretful sorrow by resigning his own see. The grave scandal caused by the mutual accusations of Spes and Bonifacius filled him with shame and anguish. These and other similar circumstances might have served as a warning that it was a hopeless attempt to enforce on all his clergy the monastic regulations of poverty, celibacy, and asceticism, which formed his own lofty ideal of a Christian life.

Augustine was a believer in dreams, prodigies, portents, miracles, the efficacy of relics, and the intercession of martyrs. In one of his sermons he details prodigies which had occurred at Jerusalem. In his *City of God*, and one of his sermons, he tells a curious story.

A relic-monger had brought from Palestine some bones, which were asserted to be those of the martyr St Stephen. They were consigned to a chapel in the church at Hippo, on which Augustine placed an inscription of four verses to tell the people of all the miracles which God had permitted to be wrought by these bones, at the reception of which he pronounced a solemn discourse.

In this sermon he mentions 'only' three dead persons by name who were recalled to life in the first two years after the arrival of the relics, but he specially narrates the miraculous recovery of Paulus and Palladia. In the Cappadocian Caesarea there was a well-known family consisting of a father and mother, seven sons, and three daughters, of whom Paulus was the sixth and Palladia the seventh.

Very shortly after the father's death all the sons were at home, and the eldest so brutally forgot himself as to violently abuse and even beat his widowed mother, while not one of her other sons interfered for her protection. In a tumult of fury the unhappy woman hastened to the baptismal font at cock-crow to curse her eldest son. There a demon, in the form of her husband's brother, met her, and asking where she was going, heard her story, and persuaded her to curse all her children alike.

'Inflamed with his viperous counsel, she prostrated herself at the font, and with dishevelled locks and bared bosom she entreated God with all her might that we might all be banished from our country, and going through all lands might terrify the whole race of men by our example.'

God heard in anger the evil prayer. During his sleep the eldest son was seized with a tremendous palsy; then within the year all the other brothers and sisters in succession were smitten with the same disease. The wretched mother, cursed by the full granting of her prayer, hanged herself. The horror-stricken children, ashamed to meet their fellow-citizens, wandered all over the Roman empire, making their misery a spectacle to all. The second brother was cured by the relics of St Lawrence at Ravenna. Paulus and Palladia went about visiting all places where miracles were performed, and became celebrated for their misery. Among other places where St Stephen performed miracles, they visited Ancona in Italy, and Uzala in Africa; but in vain.

Then on January 1, 426, Paulus saw a vision. 'A person bright to look upon, and venerable with white hair, told me that I should be cured in three months, and your Holiness' (he is addressing Augustine) 'appeared also to my sister in a vision exactly as we now see you, which signified to us that we were to come to Hippo. I too, as we passed through other cities, frequently saw your Beatitude in dreams, just as I see you now.' (Augustine, not unnaturally, was seen in dreams by various persons, and always speaks of it as if it were *really himself* who came to them, though he was unconscious of it. When he first returned to Africa the grammarian Eulogius, who had been his pupil, told him that he, while he was at Milan, had come to him in a dream, and explained a difficult passage of Cicero.) 'Admonished therefore by divine authority, we came to this city about fifteen days ago.' During this fortnight the brother and sister had frequently visited the church, and especially the memorial chapel to St Stephen, which had been built by the deacon Heraclitus, imploring God with tears to pardon their sin and restore their health. Their case had become notorious, and at Hippo they were the observed of all observers. On Easter Sunday the youth, while praying in the presence of a crowded congregation at the screen of the memorial chapel, suddenly sank in a swoon, but without the tremor which usually marked his sleep. In a short time he awoke perfectly healed before them all.

A number of persons one after another burst into the vestry to narrate the miracle to Augustine, who raised him up and kissed him. The church resounded with praises, and when silence was restored the lessons were read, and Augustine preached a short but joyous sermon, wishing the people to hear as it were only 'the eloquence of God'.

Fatigued with toils and fasting, he says that he could not have even delivered that very brief address without the help of the prayers of St Stephen, for, as Possidius tells us, he had been baptising such a multitude as would have wearied five bishops instead of one. He took Paulus home to dine with him, and requested him to put the whole story into writing.

Some days after, he placed Paulus on the steps of the pulpit with himself, and Palladia, who had not yet been healed. All the congregation could see the one perfectly cured, the other still trembling. The story of Paulus was read aloud, and it ended with a request to the people to thank God for him, and to pray for his sister. They descended from the pulpit, and Palladia went to pray before the memorial chapel. Then Augustine preached on the subject, and told the people not to honour *him*, because he had appeared to them in dreams without his own consciousness. 'Who am I? I am a mere man, one of many, not one of the great.'

While proceeding to speak of the miracles wrought in honour of St Stephen at Ancona and Uzala, he was again interrupted by shouts, 'Thanks to God! Praise to Christ!' For Palladia had hardly knelt before the screen of St Stephen's chapel than she too had sunk into a sleep and had risen healed, and was now led to the pulpit once more. For some time the emotion of the weeping congregation was intense, and Augustine could only add a very few words.

Do not these exciting scenes read as if they had occurred but yesterday at Lourdes or La Salette?

Shortly before his death Augustine narrated another miracle to Alypius. A certain Dioscurus had a daughter who became dangerously ill, and though he had been a scoffer against Christianity, he vowed to Christ that if she recovered he would become a Christian. She recovered, and he hardened his heart. He was struck with sudden blindness, and confessing his sin, promised, if his sight was restored, that he would fulfil his vow. His sight was restored, and again his heart was hardened. He was indeed received into the faith, but pretended that he could not learn the creed by heart. He was then stricken with complete paralysis, and being unable to speak, was admonished by a dream to write down a confession that this had happened to him because of his crime. After this written confession the use of all his limbs was restored, but not his power of speech; he then wrote down again that he really had the creed by heart, and still remembered it. Having thus confessed, he was finally restored.

Nay, more, Augustine himself worked miracles. When he lay ill in bed, says Possidius, a person came to him with a sick man, on whom he asked him to lay his hand and heal him. Augustine answered that if he had possessed such power he would have exercised it before. 'But,' replied the man, 'I was bidden to do this in a dream, in which someone said to me, "Go to Bishop Augustine, that he may lay hands on your sick friend, and he will be healed."' Augustine no longer hesitated, and the man went away healed. This is the only miracle directly attributed to St Augustine. It must be classed with similar incidents and similar testimonies in all ages, even down to our own. Possidius adds that, both as a presbyter and as a bishop, Augustine had often been requested to pray for persons possessed with the devil, and that when he had supplicated God with tears the demons had gone out of them.

The multiplication of these miraculous stories is one of the many proofs of the deepening superstition of the age. The miracles performed by fourth-century saints and bishops, or by the supposed bones of martyrs, in their age, stand exactly on the same level as those of the Port Royalists, or those of Edward Irving, or those wrought at the exhibitions of the Holy Coat of Trèves.

One circumstance which overwhelmed Augustine with grief was the judicial murder of his highly esteemed friend Marcellinus, who, as Imperial Commissioner, had presided over the anti-Donatist conference at Carthage. When Heraclianus, the Count of Africa, had revolted from the Emperor, and sailed with a fleet of 3000 ships to besiege Rome, he had been routed by Marinus, and afterwards executed. Marinus returned to Africa to trample out the last sparks of the rebellion, and he arrested Marcellinus and his brother, who were perfectly innocent, on the charge of having been accomplices in the rebellion. It is said that he was bribed to take this step by the Donatists, who could not forgive Marcellinus for the hostile decision which he had given at the conference. However that may be, the friends of the church, knowing the piety of Marcellinus, and grateful for the many services which he had rendered, used every exertion in his favour. Augustine wrote an earnest letter to Caecilianus, an intimate friend of Count Marinus, entreating him to use his influence to secure the liberation of the two prisoners. Caecilianus believed that he had succeeded, and Augustine began to breathe more freely. One day he visited the prisoner. The brother of Marcellinus had said to the Count, 'If I am imprisoned as a punishment for my sins, how is it that you, who are so true a Christian, have been brought into the same calamity?'

'Even supposing your kind testimony were true,' answered Marcellinus, 'is it not a divine boon that my sins should be punished on earth, and perhaps even by my blood, and not reserved for future judgement?'

Augustine, thinking that perhaps Marcellinus may have fallen in his youth into sins of impurity, affectionately urged him to penitence, if such had been the case. But Marcellinus, with a grave and modest smile, took Augustine's right hand in both of his, and said, 'I call to witness the sacraments which this hand administers, that I have never been guilty of such sin either before or after my marriage.'

Marinus, however, had determined that the brothers should die, and, anticipating that the church would interfere on behalf of Marcellinus, as she had once done on his own, he had them led out to an unusual spot on the eve of St Cyprian's Day, and there they were executed. He pretended a necessary obedience to the Emperor's command, but this was false. He was immediately recalled from Africa, and deprived of all his dignities. Augustine, overwhelmed with grief, immediately left Carthage, and Marcellinus received the honours of a martyr.

At a later period of his life another incident occurred which was a source of deep grief to Augustine. Seeing the disturbed and perilous condition of Rome before its capture by the Goths, the elder Melania had left it with her family. Like 'a Christian Sybil', Apocalypse in hand, she prophesied the coming destruction of the city. Her daughter-in-law, Albina, and Pinianus, who was married to her granddaughter the younger Melania, accompanied her in her flight. By incessant appeals and objurgations she had succeeded in inducing them to sell most of their goods, and to devote their lives to God. They were people of the highest nobility and of great wealth.

The history of the family was briefly this, as we find it in the letters of Jerome and the *Historia Lausiaca* of Palladius. The elder Melania, adopting from Jerome and other teachers the extravagant views which regarded a rupture of every public and domestic tie as a necessary part of holiness, had abandoned her young son Publicola to the care of the public praetor, and established herself in a convent on the Mount of Olives. Under the spiritual direction of Rufinus, Publicola, in spite of her neglect of her maternal duties, had grown into a good Christian and an illustrious senator. He had married Albina, daughter of the heathen Pontifex, and had two children, the young Publicola and the younger Melania. This young lady, at the age of thirteen, had been married to Pinianus, a youth of seventeen, son of a former Prefect of Africa. They had no children, and the one object of the grandmother was to separate the young people and turn them into ascetics. Their parents and all their relations strongly and unanimously opposed this suggestion, and the aged devotee had 'to fight with wild beasts', as Palladius expresses it, in order to carry her point—the wild beasts being, as he proceeds to tell us, the senators and their wives. By the force of a terrible persistence and a constant appeal to their fears, she succeeded in persuading them to sell all their goods, even a country villa which was especially dear to them. Thus their vast estates in various parts of Spain and Gaul were sold, and the proceeds distributed to the poor. They manumitted no less than 8000 slaves, retaining those only who preferred to stay with them, and they only reserved their estates in Sicily, Campania, and Africa, to support monasteries and the poor.

Melania could not, however, persuade them to bury themselves in a cloister, and after they had left Rome, she returned indignantly to Palestine, where she died within forty days in her monastery.

After a residence in Sicily, Pinianus, his wife, and Albina crossed to Africa, and spent the winter of 414 at Tagaste with the Bishop Alypius, whom they had known in Italy. The times were depressed, and the bishop, with his people, profited in every way by the piety and generosity of their noble guests. Not content with immense donations to the poor, they enriched the church of Tagaste with estates, and presented gorgeous vestments, enwoven with gold and precious stones, for the use of the presbyters. They also founded and endowed a monastery for a hundred monks, and a nunnery for one hundred and thirty virgins, together with various hospitals, so that alike the ecclesiastics and the citizens of Tagaste were highly pleased.

One of their main objects in visiting Africa had been to see Augustine, but he was unable to come to Tagaste to pay them his respects. He was getting old; his hair was white; his health was infirm. He had always been peculiarly susceptible to cold, and the winter had been severe. Further than this, he had several times incurred the censures of his people for his long absences from Hippo, though he never left them except for health, or on the affairs of the church. He tells us that his flock was always infirm and unstable; he had many detractors who never missed an opportunity of alienating from him the affections of those who seemed to love him. This state of things was very painful to him, and he wrote to the noble Romans a letter of apology, saying that though he could not then come to welcome them to Africa, he hoped that, sooner or later, he should meet them in some other city.

Under these circumstances, Pinianus and Melania came to Hippo, accompanied by Alypius. Age and ill-health prevented Albina from coming with them, and this, as the event proved, was unfortunate, for she was a person of stronger mind and calmer judgement than her daughter. If she had been with them, Pinianus might have been saved from weak compliances, and Augustine from an ordeal out of which he did not escape unblamed.

The unwarrantable practice of seizing persons against their will, and making presbyters and bishops of them, had now become chronic, and though it had succeeded well in the case of Augustine, of Paulinus, of Ambrose, and others—and doubtless also in instances where it was a sort of prearranged farce, like that which still prevails in the Coptic church—yet it was fertile of simoniacal motives and hypocritical abuse. Aware of his peril, and perhaps putting less trust in Augustine and his rude population of sailors and fishers than in his friend Alypius, Pinianus exacted from his host a pledge, in the presence of Alypius, that he would never ordain him presbyter against his will; nay, more, that he would never, by any advice or influence, press him to take orders. Pinianus had been supremely generous at Tagaste, and he knew enough of human nature to be sure that Hippo longed to share the advantages which he had bestowed upon the neighbouring diocese. Although only a fraction of his vast wealth and that of Melania was left to them it was still sufficiently ample to excite cupidity, and this cupidity was still further inflamed by the benefactions which he now gave to Augustine, and which the bishop divided among the clergy, the monks, and the poor.

The people of Hippo had thus as it were 'tasted blood', and a plot was got up—in which there is reason to fear that some of the beneficiaries among the monks and clergy had a large share—to secure the advantage which would accrue to the city from the permanent residence of the noble and wealthy devotees. Why should all that stream of gold flow into the coffers of the church of Tagaste? If Alypius and the people of Tagaste had forgone the blessed opportunity of securing a millionaire and a patrician for their presbyterate, so much better was the chance for Hippo. Who could be very scrupulous when the object in view was so pious?

Whenever a man became a presbyter or a bishop public opinion expected, and indeed at Hippo demanded, that he should at once give up his entire possessions to the common good of the church. Augustine indeed had openly proclaimed to the people that he would neither admit anyone among the body of his clergy, nor retain him in it, unless he succumbed to this exacting and autocratic regulation. Here then was a chance for the monks, the clerics, the paupers of this turbulent town. Estates in Sicily, estates in Campania, estates in Africa—all this wealth would become the ecclesiastical property of the Christians at Hippo, and they would number a descendant of the noblest families of Rome among their ministers, if they could only be successful in one pious coup d'état!

They seized their opportunity, and all the circumstances are frankly described to us by Augustine himself. At one of the church assemblies Pinianus, Melania, and Alypius were present, and there was a great throng of people. Augustine was seated in his episcopal chair at the end of the apse, and Pinianus felt himself secure in the promise he had received. The bishop, however, had not yet dismissed the catechumens, when there began to arise a great shout, 'Pinianus for presbyter! Pinianus for presbyter!' Augustine at first behaved worthily of himself. He rose from his seat, advanced to the choir-screen, and said to the people, 'I have promised Pinianus that he shall not be ordained against his will. If you ordain him I will resign my bishopric.' Having said this he again retired to his seat. For a moment, but for a moment only, the conspiracy was checked. It broke out again like a suppressed flame, because, he tells us, the people either hoped to force him to break his promise, or at any rate to force Alypius to ordain his guest. Some of the leading members of the congregation now mounted the steps of the choir and tried to persuade him to yield, but he said, 'I will not break my word to Pinianus, nor will I suffer any other bishop to ordain him without my express permission. Even if I did permit it, I should still be breaking my pledge. Besides, a forcible ordination will but drive him away from Hippo and from Africa.'

But the hot-blooded and self-interested mob were now too much infuriated to listen to reason, and Augustine—not to his credit, as he himself must have felt—began to waver and to lose his head. The people pressed upon Alypius with dangerous menaces, accusing him of the very greed of which they themselves were now so flagrantly guilty. 'You want to keep Pinianus to yourself,' they shouted, 'that you may dip your hands in his purse.' Augustine was overwhelmed with shame when he heard the gross insults with which, in his own cathedral church, his unruly flock assailed a brother bishop whom he esteemed and loved. He admits that the tumult terrified and confused him, and he afterwards entreated the prayers of Alypius that he might be forgiven. He felt extreme alarm lest Alypius and his friends should suffer personal violence in his very presence, and he was so paralysed by the dread of the church being wrecked by the baser part of the mob that he was ready to catch at any straw. He would not indeed say one word to influence the decision of Pinianus, but on the other hand it remains a blot on his courage and on his character that he did not ascend his pulpit—as a Chrysostom would have done, and did, under similar circumstances—and repress the violence of these simonists by his immense personal authority. He thought of leaving the church, but feared that, if he did, murder might take place; nor could he even venture to go out side by side with Alypius—which would have necessarily ended the whole scene—lest one of the rioters should assault him. He sat on his episcopal throne overwhelmed with grief and incapable of decision, when a sudden message from Pinianus, brought to him by one of his monks, seemed to offer a loophole of escape. Pinianus sent to tell him that, if he were forced into ordination, he would take an oath to leave Africa, which would render their greedy violence of no avail.

Augustine again showed weakness. He would not announce the message to the people for fear of infuriating them yet more; but as Pinianus entreated his protection, he left the apse where he was sitting and came to him. Meanwhile the young Roman, who also showed timidity, had sent him a second message by another monk, named Timasius—and it is a suspicious circumstance that these monks, who would have been the chief gainers by his bounty, seem to have been swarming round him (Augustine says that he could not find that any of the monks or clergy were in the plot)—that he was willing to swear further that he would remain at Hippo if he were not ordained by force. Could there be a more transparent proof of the fact that the violence which in such cases was often represented as an impulse of the Holy Spirit was dictated by greed alone?

The message came to Augustine like a refreshing breeze in the midst of his perplexity. He hurried as fast as he could to Alypius to tell him of this new promise, thinking, he says, that he ought to prefer the acceptance of a spontaneous offer to the destruction of his church. Alypius, however, knowing what he owed to his friends, and also that Augustine was responsible for maintaining order and protecting them, curtly refused to give any advice. Then Augustine felt bound to mount the pulpit and tell the people what Pinianus had promised. They, however (so disinterested was their desire that he should be ordained!), after a little muttering among themselves, wanted him to add the oath that, if ever he consented to ordination, it should be at Hippo only. They could trust themselves to force further confessions out of him at a later time. Pinianus agreed; the people demanded an oath; but here Pinianus wavered again. 'How if necessary circumstances should force him to leave Hippo? How if there should be an invasion of Goths? How,' added Melania, 'if there should be a plague?' but this last suggestion was rejected by her husband. 'I dare not suggest the possibility of an invasion to the people,' answered Augustine; 'it would be a bad omen, and would look like an excuse.' It was decided, however, to try the popular feelings on the subject, and no sooner had he come to the words 'necessary circumstances' than there rose a shout, and the tumult recommenced. Pinianus again gave way and persuaded Augustine to come forward with him, in spite of fatigue, and to stand by his side.

The oath that he would stay at Hippo unconditionally—an oath disgraceful to the people and discreditable to Augustine himself, who had thus seen the rights of hospitality violated in his presence—was publicly taken. The people shouted 'God be thanked!' and demanded that the oath should be signed by Pinianus. The catechumens were dismissed. Then the people, by the mouths of the faithful, begged the two bishops to subscribe also. Augustine took the stylus, and had half written his name, when Melania interfered, and prevented him from finishing it. Augustine tells us that he could not imagine what difference it would make, but the lady probably wished to save him from what she not unnaturally regarded as a permanent disgrace. She and her husband openly complained that the whole scene, ending as it did in the deplorable fiasco of extorting from a Roman patrician, in a church, and in the presence of two bishops, an enforced oath that he would live in a particular town, was nothing more nor less than a piece of brigandage, all the more infamous because it was hypocritical.

Augustine evidently felt some pangs of conscience. He was sensible of the disgrace, and admitted the violence, only trying (and very unsuccessfully) to shelter his people from the charge of greedy hypocrisy. Alypius, deeply and justly offended by the menaces and insults which had been addressed to him, at once left Hippo, and soon afterwards Pinianus secretly followed him. This gave the people of Hippo an opportunity for fresh riots, to which they added the publication of disgraceful calumnies.

Whether Pinianus merely claimed the right of any other citizen to go and return when he liked, or whether he doubted the cogency of a forced oath, is uncertain. The latter had probably something to do with it, for Alypius wrote a dignified but reproachful letter to Augustine, in which he mentioned this as a question to be discussed, and argued that at any rate Pinianus was not to be treated as if he were a public slave.

Albina was much more outspoken. She upbraided Augustine with not having kept a promise which he had distinctly made. She charged his people with barefaced greed in their desire to keep her son-in-law among them either as a presbyter or as a rich layman, in order that they might be the gainers in money by what she did not hesitate to call his 'exile' or 'relegation', or even his 'deportation'; and she too asked whether he was bound to keep an oath which had been simply wrung out of him by force. Augustine replied that no one would believe the oath of a bishop, or anyone else, if it were not regarded as binding in all cases; but the extreme weakness of his reply to Albina's plain-speaking—for which he thanked her—seems to show that, though not guilty of any share in the gross misconduct of his people, he felt in his conscience that he had acted with a lack of firmness of which his friends had good right to complain.

How the affair ended we do not know. If Pinianus felt himself bound to return to Hippo it must have been with feelings of the deepest disgust. It is probable that Augustine prevailed on the people of Hippo to liberate Pinianus from an oath which testified to their disgrace and his own pusillanimity. Perhaps the young Roman lost the remainder of his property from the violent exactions of Count Heraclion, and when he was reduced to poverty there was no more reason for detaining him. However that may be, it is certain that a year or two later Albina, Pinianus, and Melania were with Jerome in Palestine. They wrote to ask the advice of Augustine about a discussion which they had held with Pelagius, and also sent him kind messages through Jerome. We are glad to know that they were reconciled after so severe a grievance. Probably Augustine did not so readily forgive himself. Deprived of all things, the husband and wife at last separated. Melania died seven years after in a convent—perhaps that founded by her grandmother—in Jerusalem. Pinianus became the abbot of a little community of thirty monks.

13

Last Days

Besides his private griefs, which were many and severe, Augustine, in common with all his Western contemporaries, was afflicted by the perils and miseries of his time. The perpetual advance of the hordes of barbarians, and the many intrigues, infamies, murders, and seditions, which marked the reigns of the feeble Arcadius and the yet feebler Honorius, were a perpetual source of terror. Stilicho was the one bulwark of the West, and even before his disgraceful assassination Jerome was openly and secretly sneering at him because he was by birth a half-barbarian. When Stilicho was murdered there was nothing to defend Rome from its destruction by Alric on August 24, 410. That tremendous event forced Jerome to cry, 'O God, the heathen have come into thine inheritance.'

Augustine felt no less deeply the horror of the time. In 409, distressed beyond measure by the wars and rumours of wars on every side, and the alarm caused by the Circumcellions in the diocese of Hippo, the presbyter Victorinus had written to ask him for counsel and consolation. What was he to think of, what answer was he to give to, the taunts of pagans, when news kept coming in of monks being massacred and consecrated virgins seized by ruffians? Augustine answered that the sins of pagans

and Christians alike deserved punishment, but that those
of pagans, who knew not God's will, were less flagrant than
those of Christians, who knew it. The Christians of that
day could not, he said, match themselves with men like
Daniel and the Maccabees, who yet had to suffer great
calamities and confessed to God that they deserved them.
Let Victorinus take refuge in prayer and duty. The seizure
of virgins might even redound to God's glory. Thus a niece
of Severus, Bishop of Sitifa, had been captured by barbarians, and immediately three brothers of the house in
which she was kept as a captive fell grievously ill. The
mother entreated the captive virgin to pray for them,
promising that if they recovered she should be restored to
her parents. She prayed and fasted and was heard. The
barbarians returned her with honour and uninjured to her
own family.

But if we ask how it was that imperial Rome bowed herself into the dust before hordes of rude barbarians,
beneath her by an immeasurable inferiority in all but courage and manhood, the answer is that on the one hand
paganism was effete with an absolute decrepitude, and
that Christianity, as it was then understood and in part
perverted, did not supply the old heroism and battle-brunt
which enables every living nation to find an impenetrable
bulwark in the strong arms of her sons. The energies of
Christians in the fourth century were no longer political or
national. The Christian Emperors, except Theodosius,
were for the most part feeble and wretched puppets in the
hands of bigots, women, eunuchs, and priests. The popular form of Christianity was monastic and superstitious. It
cooled the patriotism or hampered the energies of statesmen and warriors. The pure stream of the gospel was
rendered turbid by unnatural and effeminating influences, and ecclesiastical dominance was ill fitted to preserve social order. There was too indiscriminate a mixture
of civil and sacerdotal interests.

'Men forgot strong virtues for monachal abstinences,

their country for the cloister, and war for controversy. The age of theological splendour was the prelude of barbarism. So true is it that religion, a divine support for the human soul, is not an all-sufficing instrument for politics, and cannot supply for any nation the need of freedom and of toil' (Villemain). We must not, however, forget that if Christianity helped to destroy the empire, it helped also to rebuild it on truer foundations. 'The Roman empire,' says Montalembert, 'without the barbarians, was an abyss of servitude and corruption. The barbarians without the monks were chaos. The barbarians and the monks united recreated a world which was to be called Christendom.'

After the capture of Rome, Augustine preached several times to his people on that subject, and the circumstance which most afflicted him was the ground which it gave to pagans to set down all these catastrophes to the anger of their offended gods against the votaries of the new religion. This was the theme of the last pagan historians Eunapius and Zosimus, and of the last Christian poet Merbaudes. It was the desire to refute this taunt which gave occasion to Augustine's greatest book, the *City of God*. The rule of divine providence over the world and man was the central conception which Augustine desired to illustrate. Augustine meant to address the work to his friend Marcellinus, but his judicial murder took place in 413, before he had finished the second book.

When finished the *De Civitate Dei* occupied twenty-two books, and though he began it 'in a flame of zeal for God' against the blasphemies of the pagans, it was often interrupted by other duties. In his *Retractations* he tells us that the first five books were meant to refute polytheism, and the charges brought by its defenders against the supposed perils caused by Christianity. The second five books were addressed to those who, admitting that human catastrophes had occurred and would occur in all ages, said that polytheism was necessary to secure the happiness of the future life.

The remaining twelve books are positive, and not, like the first ten, mainly negative. They contrast the two cities—the city of God and the city of the world—in their origin (11–14), in their development (15–18), and in their final destiny (19–22). The whole book deals with the two cities, but receives its name from the true and eternal City of God. Many such books have since been written, notably the great *Discours sur l'histoire universelle* of Bossuet; but the conception of so grand a design is due to the fertile brain of the Bishop of Hippo. The opening words, *Gloriosissimam Civitatem Dei*, are, as has been truly said, a keynote to the whole book. It is Augustine's conception of what a history of the church should be, as well as of the lessons which he learnt from the manifestation of God in the history of the world. It abounds in erudition and in eloquence.

His argument throughout the earlier books resembles that in the Book of Wisdom. He says that sorrows and calamities fall alike on Christians and heathens, but that their effect is different. The fire that melts the gold hardens the clay; the fire that purges the wheat destroys the chaff. God means the trials of Christians to be for their blessing and amelioration, those of heathens to be for their punishment. Rome had become half pagan during its siege by Alaric, and even when Rome was nothing but a pagan city it had been taken by the Gauls and burnt by Nero. And, after all, the conquerors of Rome on this occasion, though heretics, were still Christians. Thanks to the brave Arian bishop Ulfilas, they had the Bible in their hands. Augustine was awed by the fall of Rome, but it did not cause him anything like the horror and distress which it caused Jerome. He regarded it, in fact, as a divine judgement upon a decrepit paganism.

In these books he gives a sweeping survey of the Roman empire and its history, to prove that selfishness was its ruling principle. Then he examines the general idea of heathenism, exposes its deep-seated corruption, and identifies its deities with demons. On the other hand, he finds the centre of Christianity in Christ himself, and traces it through the sacred history. Finally he ends the entire aeon of mortality in an eternal dualism—the unchangeable and irremediable separation of the bad from the good. His whole philosophy of history reduces itself to an irreconcilable antagonism. The city of evil is left to its own fate. Its very virtues are unworthy of praise. The beauty and profundity of Greek literature, the earnestness with which philosophers had knocked at the doors of truth, the splendid instances of virtue and self-sacrifice which illuminate the early history of the Roman republic, nay, even the fact that his own conception of God came mainly from neo-Platonistic teachers, might have sufficed to show him that his fundamental conception was narrow and imperfect. Humanity is the same everywhere. Its elements are identical in the evil and the good, and as the good often triumphs in the individual man it triumphs also even in the heathen world.

Even in this great work we find the taint of the Manichean conceptions in which Augustine had been so long entangled. God is one, not two. Throughout his whole universe with equal love he makes his sun to shine on the evil and on the good, and sends rain on the just and on the unjust. It is a world in which even while we were yet sinners Christ died for all; Christ died for the ungodly. Nor does Augustine touch on the deep failure of the church of God itself, so far as it is a visible community, although it was becoming so degenerate that thirty years later Salvian called it not a *placatrix* but an *exacerbatrix Dei*. But still the *Civitas Dei* is a splendid monument to the genius of the writer, and a landmark in the progress of history. It contains a Christian philosophy of history, imperfect, indeed, and in many respects mistaken, yet strikingly suggestive. 'It is the funeral oration of the Roman empire pronounced in a cloister; the interpretation of the past by the new genius which changed the world.' It illustrates in a very marked degree the difference between the old order and the new.

It shows how in the new belief the interests of the City of God had superseded those of the empire, and 'all the moral energy which remained in the civilised world was turned toward pious contemplation, and yielded the empire to the barbarians.'

Augustine had more and more need, as the years darkened round him, to take refuge in the thoughts and hopes which he has enshrined in this his greatest work. At the time of the conference against the Donatists, Alaric was preparing to invade Africa, and fix at Carthage the seat of a new empire. A storm destroyed his fleet in the short voyage between Rhegium and Messina, and he died. The ruin of that smiling land and of its flourishing church was destined to be accomplished by Genseric, a barbarian far less generous and more ruthless than the conqueror of Rome. The fortunes of Hippo and of all Africa were involved in the conduct of a man whom Augustine had loved and honoured, and were the indirect and unforeseen result of advice which he himself had innocently given.

This man was Count Bonifacius, who is praised both by pagan and Christian historians, and who with his treacherous friend and rival Aetius is called by Procopius 'the last of the Romans'. Augustine and Alypius alike regarded him as a sincere Christian, and more than once he seemed on the point of forsaking the world in which he occupied so splendid a position, and turning monk. Shortly after the death of his wife he met the two bishops at Tubunae, and told them his desire to abandon war and public life, and to occupy himself with the combat against demons in the saintly solitude of a monastery. They dissuaded him from his purpose, and told him that he could best serve the church by repressing the incursions of barbarians and helping to crush the schism of the Donatists. The advice proved supremely fatal to themselves, to Boniface, to Africa, to the whole Roman empire. This was in 417. But for that quiet interview between the warlike Count and the

Christian bishops there might have been a difference in the history of the world.

In 422 Boniface was sent to fight under Castinus against the Vandals in Spain, and he would probably have defeated them entirely, had he not thrown up his command in disgust at the arrogant incompetence of his commander. He returned to Ostia, and thence to Africa. During the brief usurpation of John he held Africa for the Empress-Regent Placidia and her young son Valentinian III, who had taken refuge at Constantinople. This procured him the highest honour, but also the extreme envy of Felix, the master of the soldiers, who with his wife Padusa and a deacon named Grunitus ruled the palace. Aetius, too—a Sarmatian who had risen to the highest military rank in the Roman army, and had great influence over the Huns, among whom he had lived as a hostage—was jealous of Boniface, though they had once been brothers in arms.

The count had been sent by Placidia on an embassy to the Vandals of Baetica. They were virulent and persecuting Arians, and at the Vandal court Boniface met and wooed his second wife, a beautiful and wealthy Spanish lady named Pelagia, who was a niece of Genseric. She was an Arian. He thought that he had won her over to the Nicene faith, but unhappily he was mistaken. The house of Boniface began to be filled by Arians. His daughter was baptised by an Arian bishop, and to the intense horror of the African church some Christian virgins were also rebaptised by the heretics. These circumstances increased the jealousy and suspicion which were carefully fostered by the rivals of Boniface at the court, and Aetius advised Placidia to send for him, while at the same time he sent to the count a secret message that if he came he would be assassinated. Boniface refused to come, and prepared for war. At first successful in his revolt, he was afterwards defeated, and meanwhile Africa was plunged in unspeakable miseries. His soldiers had to be maintained as well as the imperial armies. The tribes of Mount Atlas seized the opportunity given them by these distractions to rush down on the defenceless country. Harvests were burnt and trampled, towns destroyed, churches pillaged. Terror and desolation reigned on every side.

Full of anguish, Augustine at last found an opportunity to write to his former friend. The character of Boniface had deteriorated in every way, and it was even rumoured that he had not only broken his vow of continence by his second marriage, but had plunged into gross licentiousness. All that could be urged by a Christian bishop was expressed by Augustine with pathetic eloquence and earnest appeal.

Alas! it was now too late to recall Boniface to his former state of mind. Unable to hold his own against the native tribes of Africa on the one side, and the imperial forces on the other, he turned traitor to his own country, and let loose the whirlwind by summoning the Vandals to his assistance. In May 428, 50,000 wild Vandals, Alans, and Goths landed in Africa under their king Genseric. They had been carried over from Spain in the ships of Boniface, and in two years became masters of the province, which they held for a century. They at once made common cause with the native Mauretanians and the Donatist Circumcellions, and they all turned their common hatred against the church. Then followed scenes of unspeakable horror which Possidius and others have described. Armed with weapons of all kinds, the brutal hosts of barbarians poured themselves over that smiling land which had been for so many ages the granary of Rome.

Victor Vitensis gives us a frightful picture of this Vandal invasion. Towns were destroyed and their inhabitants massacred or scattered abroad; churches were deprived of their ministers, of whom some had been slain with tortures, others by the sword, while a yet more wretched number had been driven to apostasy, and had become the slaves of their Arian captors. Hymns and praises were heard no more, and in most places the churches themselves had been reduced to ashes. The sacraments were no longer administered, for none sought them. Many had fled into forests and mountain caves, where they died of hunger and privation. Bishops and clergy, no longer able to help the poor, were themselves reduced to indigence and even to beggary. Three cities only—Carthage, Hippo, and Cirta—were able to hold out for a time. Augustine sometimes solaced himself with the remark which he heard from some wise man 'that a man could hardly be great who felt surprise that timbers and stones fall or that mortals die'; but every gleam of happiness had vanished from his life. Tears were his food day and night, while men daily said unto him, 'Where is thy God?'

But misery did not make him neglect his duty. He preached frequently to his terrified and despairing people, and did his best to advise and teach them if he could not alleviate their miseries. When Quodvultdeus wrote to ask him what congregations and their ministers ought to do when hard pressed by the enemy, he replied that if the people wished to fly into fortified places it was not for the bishops to forbid them, but they ought themselves to abide by the flocks and churches as long as it remained in their power to discharge any of the duties of their office.

Honoratius, Bishop of Thiave, wrote to ask what use it was for bishops to stay merely to witness deeds of massacre and outrage which they could not hinder, and to be tortured to death for not delivering up treasures which they did not possess. He gave the same reply as to Quodvultdeus, and when Honoratius quoted to him the command of Christ, 'When they persecute you in one city, flee to another,' he wrote back to say that there were but two circumstances in which he considered the flight of a bishop to be justifiable—one, as in the case of Athanasius and Cyprian, when only the bishop was attacked, and his sacred functions could be discharged by those who were not persecuted; and the other, when all their people have left them. Otherwise, no bishop ought ever to leave his

people at the very time when they most needed his ministrations. Nor did Augustine neglect his controversial duties
even in these days of labour, trouble, rebuke, and blas-
phemy. He answered the books of Julian of Eclanum. He
wrote against and disputed with the Arians whom the Vandal irruption had once more brought into prominence. He
continued, but in a tone of unwonted mildness, his arguments against the Semi-Pelagian monks of Marseilles. At
the request of Quodvultdeus he even began a book on
heresies, which he was never able to finish.

When Count Darius was sent from Ravenna to try and
restore peace Augustine helped him with his best advice,
and exchanged with him a pleasant correspondence, during which he sent to Darius some of his books and received
from him some valuable medicines. The visit of Darius put
an end to many delusions. Boniface showed him the
treacherous letter of Aetius which had driven him into
rebellion, and he became reconciled to Placidia, who was
now alarmed by the ambitious designs of Aetius. Boniface
endeavoured to undo the frightful mischief which he had
caused. He offered Genseric a vast sum of money if he
would retire to Spain; but Genseric laughed in his face.
Then he tried threats, which were equally unsuccessful. At
last he took up arms against the Vandals to whom he had
betrayed the most necessary province of the empire. But
his old success had deserted him. He was defeated and
driven into Hippo, which was at once besieged by Genseric
both by land and sea. This was at the beginning of June
430.

Augustine was now surrounded in his monastery by a
number of bishops who had fled from the conflagration of
their churches and the ruin of their cities. Among them
was his biographer, Possidius, who had enjoyed his
friendship for forty years. They all wept and fasted and
prayed together, imploring God to help them under this
terrible tribulation. 'I have but one prayer to God amid
these calamities,' said Augustine to them; 'either that he

would set free this city from the enemy, or if not, that he would make his servants strong to bear his will, or at least that he would take me to himself from this world.'

Towards the end of August, when the siege had lasted three months, he fell ill, and was able to preach no more. He had often told his friends that no baptised Christian, not even the saintliest bishop, ought to leave this life without a worthy and ample penitence. He acted up to his ideal. As soon as he felt that the fever was dangerous he had the seven penitential psalms written out for him in large letters and hung on the walls around his bed, that he might be able constantly to read them. Ten days before he died he begged his friends to visit him no more, except when the physicians came, or his food was brought to him. He spent his whole days in prayer and meditation, untroubled by any earthly business. He had no will to make, for he had no possessions to leave, and several years before he had commended to his people the choice of his valued presbyter Heraclius as his successor in the see of Hippo. The end of his busy and troubled life was at hand, though he was in full possession of sight, hearing, and all his faculties. He died on August 28, 430, in the seventy-sixth year of his age, and the thirty-fifth of his episcopate. From early manhood to old age he had lived in the service of his church.

In June of the following year the Vandals abandoned the siege from want of supplies. Boniface, who had received reinforcements from Rome and Constantinople, once more fought a pitched battle with them. He was defeated, and returned to Italy, where in 432 he fell by the lance-thrust of Aetius. Hippo was deserted by its inhabitants, and burnt to the ground by the Vandals. The only thing which escaped the conflagration was the library which Augustine had consecrated to the use of the church. Carthage fell before the Vandals in 439. The church of northern Africa was destroyed, and the country fell back into a desolation and barbarism from which it has never fully emerged. Augustine was spared the anguish of witnessing the final destruction of the city which he had loved so long and the church which he had served so faithfully. He had done his day's work, and God sent him sleep.

He was the last Bishop of Hippo. The people escaped by sea, and in the seventh century the town ceased to exist. When he died there were five hundred Catholic bishops in the province. Not twenty years later there seem to have been only eighteen.

Not long ago Bona fell into the hands of the French, and it has been proposed to build a cathedral over the supposed site of Augustine's grave. He is still traditionally remembered in the neighbourhood as *Rumi Kebir*, 'the great Christian'.

14

Theology

Augustine had been endowed by God with a rich and many-sided nature, and his life was extraordinarily full of the most varied labours. In him a heart glowing like that of the cherubim, and an intellect keen, subtle, and casuistical as that of a schoolman, acted and reacted upon each other, and lent their combined force to an African nature, passionate as that of Tertullian, and a will of indomitable energy and persistence. And these elements of his temperament were powerfully affected by the moral and intellectual history of his life. It was a life of violent reaction from violent extremes of practice and of theory. He had plunged at an early age into sensual dissipation, from which at one bound he passed into an exaggerated estimate of the intrinsic value of monastic asceticism. He had lived in haughty self-reliance; the reaction, aided by controversy, had carried him into a conception of God which annihilated the freedom of the human will. As a Manichee he had appealed exclusively to the reason, and after a brief interspace of scepticism and neo-Platonism (each of which left its own influence), he ended by an extravagant reliance on external authority. The varying phases of his life, the oscillations of opinion which necessitated many subsequent rehandlings, the sporadic manner in which his opinions were expressed, the extent to which they were modified by the dialectic exigencies of incessant polemical encounters, render it difficult to frame any exact system from his writings.

Hence the most opposite parties—Reformers and Romanists, Jensenists and Jesuits, the adherents of Molina and those of Bajus, the admirers of Petavius and those of Calixt, Sacramentarians and Zwinglians, Tridentines and Anglicans—have alike claimed his authority. He profoundly influenced writers so unlike each other as Erigena and Anselm, Aquinas and Bonaventura. Luther seized on his doctrine of justification, Calvin on his theory of predestination, the schoolmen on his systematising methods, the mystics on his burning spirit of devotion, the Popes on his idea of the church. He anticipated some of the views and arguments alike of Descartes, of Leibniz, and of Butler; he is at once the founder of scholasticism and the first of the Western mystics.

It is not easy to state with any exactitude the opinion of Augustine about the sacraments. He regarded baptism as a necessary condition of salvation, and it almost seems as if he attributed to it an *ex opere operato* validity. Of the Lord's Supper he speaks partly as the sacrament of unity with the body of Christ and partly as a sacrifice. In the first aspect the Holy Communion is the sacrament of incorporation in the church, which he defines as Christ's body diffused throughout the world. He does not regard the Eucharist as *the sacrifice of Christ's actual body* (of which there seems to be no trace in Augustine's works), but the sacrifice by the church *of herself* as the body of Christ.

The only shadow of a complete system which he has left is in his brief *Enchiridion* to Laurentius. But in all his works he deals more (except so far as mere occasional words go) with God and with man—with theology and anthropology—than with the special work of Christ. He does indeed deal in a practical manner with the doctrine of the Trinity, but his main thought is the transcendent supremacy, and, so to speak, aloofness, of God, which he had learnt in no small measure from the neo-Platonists. He exalts God's decree to the absolute annihilation of any real human freedom. Hence his hamartiology—the doctrine of sin to which he devoted so much elaborate discussion—is radically vitiated; and his soteriology—his doctrine of a saviour—though so orthodox that his very words were largely adopted by the Council of Chalcedon, was reduced to practical impotence. Augustine's saviour is not the saviour of the world. He is only the saviour of the church, and even in the church itself the saviour only of a mere handful of the elect, whom he saves only under strictly ecclesiastical conditions. It is the church, not the living Christ, which becomes in the Augustinian system the one mediator between God and man.

This, in fact, is the worst blot upon Augustine's theology. Much as he speaks of Christ, he robs him of his most divine prerogatives. So far from being the redeemer of all mankind, he becomes a mere instrument which enabled God to carry out for a very small number in a very small church a predestination to individual election, entirely apart from any merit or demerit of their own.

Unhappily, Augustine, though a marvellously acute and subtle, was not a consecutive or homogeneous thinker, but developed, and sometimes improvised, his convictions according to polemical needs. In his argument with the Manicheans he never lost his tendency to pessimism, while in his controversy with the Donatists he had elaborated his church system, and in that with the Pelagians he had thought out the novelties about predestination and original sin. An external fact—Adam's single sin—had, by some unique quality of its own, so totally depraved, distorted, vitiated, and poisoned the whole nature of all his millions of descendants in all ages, that they were incapable of any good whatever, and could only be changed by an external act, baptism, which was so indispensable that every person dying unbaptised is eternally lost; and even infants dying unbaptised cannot be saved. The result is that mankind as a whole is a lost and condemned mass, doomed, even before they were born, to endless agonies. He says that punishments are not meant to purify but ever to illustrate the divine justice; that it would not be unjust if all men were eternally punished, but that a very few are saved to illustrate the divine mercy. It has often been said that Augustine was overshadowed to the last by the Manicheism of his early manhood. Wesley, though he had little sympathy with Augustine, yet saw that he was no Calvinist.

Naturally, therefore, an almost unfathomable cleft was drawn by the new Pharisaism between the so-called secular and the so-called religious life. In the developments of this system, marriage and the possession of property were half-tolerated, half-disparaged; and utterly anti-scriptural views both of God and of life gave the name of 'religious' or 'servants of God' only to monks, or virgins, or those who gave up their lives to an austere, morbid, and unnatural self-maceration. The theology of Augustine, and hence also that of the Middle Ages, was penetrated through and through with dualism, and for the majority of the human race with practical despair.

To all this scholastic rigidity of formal doctrines and burdensome concentration on the will he was partly swept by the currents of superstition, and partly driven step by step by the confidence in his own inferential logic under the stress of never-ending disputes. Augustine was so incessantly occupied with proving the countless errors of individuals and of sects, that he came to regard theology as a series of propositions as clear and exactly definable as those of Euclid. Mozley says: 'He did not allow the unity and simplicity of his answers to be at all interfered with by large and inclusive views of truth. To the extreme contradictory on the one side he gave the extreme contradictory on the other.' The gate of the church began to bristle with a framework of finely-articulated dogmas, many of them arrived at by pure sophistry, defended with hard intolerance, and enforced by sheer authority.

In each of his chief controversies he mingled a great error with great truths. The Manichees, and not he, were right when they refused to regard the Romish episcopal community as the depository of all truth. The Donatists were right, and not he, when they denied that the church was justified in resorting to persecution. The Pelagians were in the right, and not he, when they refused to admit an unmixed corruption and absolute depravity of human nature as the result of Adam's sin.

And of the true nature of the church Augustine had a very narrow conception. He confounded the church mainly with the clergy, and dwarfed the ideal of Christ into the founder of the dwindled church instead of the saviour of all mankind. He had not entered into the large conception of that church of Christ into which many were to come from the east and from the west, from the north and from the south—of that church in which there were many folds and many mansions—above all, of that church to which belong vast multitudes of those who are not ostensibly within its pale. The church as represented by Ambrose overawed his wavering scepticism by its authoritative claim to be the sole possessor of truth.

The church to him was an external establishment, subjected to the autocracy of bishops, largely dependent on the opinion of Rome. It was a church represented almost exclusively by a sacerdotal caste, devoted to the aggrandisement of its own power, cut off by celibacy from ordinary human interests, armed with fearful spiritual weapons, and possessing the sole right to administer a grace which came magically through none but mechanical channels.

And this church might, nay was bound to, *enforce* the acceptance of its own dogmas and customs even in minute details and in outward organisation. It was justified in enforcing unity by using the arm of the state to fetter free consciences by cruel persecution. And outside this church, with its many abuses, its few elect, its vast masses arbitrarily

doomed to certain destruction, its acknowledged multitude of ambitious, greedy, ignorant, and unworthy
priests—there was no salvation! Augustine substituted an
organised church and a supernatural hierarchy for an
ever-present Christ. To Augustine more than anyone is
due the theory which was most prolific of the abiding curse
inflicted on many generations by an arrogant and usurp-
ing priestcraft.

The outward church of Augustine was Judaic, not
Christian. The whole Epistle to the Hebrews is a protest
against it. And all that was most deplorable in this theology
and ecclesiasticism became the most cherished heritage of
the church of the Middle Ages in exact proportion to its
narrowest ignorance, its tyrannous ambition, its moral corruption, and its unscrupulous cruelty.

But though Augustinianism triumphed in the church, it
did not triumph without protest, nor did it triumph completely. Vehement as were his attacks on the Pelagians, the
Greek church could not be induced to share his opinions.
Two synods—those of Jerusalem and Diospolis—accepted
the explanations of Pelagius, and one Pope, Zosimus, until
he was frightened into changing sides, not only declared
his innocence but rebuked his opponents. Theodore of
Mopsuestia, the greatest exegete of the ancient church,
rejected Augustine's doctrine of original sin, and charged
him with teaching ignoble thoughts of God which even
human justice would condemn. Vincent of Lerins, whose
definition of what is Catholic in doctrine has become
proverbial, drew it up as a test which sufficed for the rejec-
tion of Augustine's novelties, since they had hitherto been
held never, nowhere, and by none.

The extreme view of predestination, and of God as
arbitrary will, belongs rather to Calvinism than to Christian doctrine. The notion that mercy is only a form of
divine egoism, which has in view God's glory, not man's
happiness, is more Muhammadan than Catholic. The doctrine of endless torments for all but the few, to which he

first gave fixity in opposition to the opinion then prevalent even in the Western church, has ever been confronted by God's revelation of himself as a God of love to the individual soul. As in Calvin and Jonathan Edwards, the blessed are to be indifferent if not delighted spectators of these torments. How different was the whole system of Augustine from that of Origen! The system of Origen is mainly occupied with God and hope; that of Augustine with punishment and sin. Origen yearns for a final unity, Augustine acquiesces in an eternal dualism. Origen can scarcely bear the thought that even the devil should be unsaved; Augustine is undisturbed in contemplating the endless torments of nearly all mankind! Semi-Pelagianism, in spite of his arguments, has been and is the general doctrine of the Christian church.

Happily there was another and a far brighter side to the religious work of his life. As a bishop he diligently ruled his church; as a preacher he surpassed all his contemporaries in practical usefulness; as a metaphysician he anticipated some of the best thoughts of Leibniz and Malebranche. We may deplore the extremes of his theology, but the whole world has gained from the example of his holiness and the outpourings of his religious genius. He was a mystic as well as a schoolman, and shows a rare combination of passionate fervour with intrepid dogmatism and dialectical subtlety. If the ambitious priest, and ruthless inquisitor, and hard predestinarian, can claim his authority for much that obscures the mercy of God and darkens the life of man, on the other hand he has supported the faith and brightened the love of thousands who have been ignorant of his church theories, and totally uninfluenced by his theological dogmatism.

He was less firm than Athanasius, less learned than Jerome, less eloquent than Chrysostom, less profound than Gregory of Nazianzus, less clear-sighted than Theodore of Mopsuestia, less forcible in administration than Basil or Ambrose; yet in universality of grasp, in the combination of brilliant qualities, and in the intensity of personal religious conviction, he surpassed them all. No pagan of his day can for a moment be compared to him. He was the last great man of Africa, and after him the reign of barbarism commenced.

In art, the special attribute of Augustine is a transpierced or flaming heart, to show his ardent devotion and poignant repentance. One of the famous subjects of his life is his vision of the child Jesus trying to empty the ocean into a hole in the sands to rebuke Augustine for endeavouring to fathom the mystery of the Trinity. This subject has been exquisitely treated by Murillo, and in Garofalo's picture in our National Gallery, and by Albrecht Dürer, Rubens, Van Dyck, and Raphael. Of modern pictures in which he is introduced the most famous is that by Ary Scheffer in 1845, which represents him at the window in Ostia with his mother Monnica. See Mrs Jameson's *Sacred and Legendary Art*, i.308–315.

Appendix

Works of Augustine

Augustine was a prolific writer. Even in his *Retractations* he mentions 93 works, in 232 books, and this does not include all his writings, nor his numerous letters and sermons. His works fall into no less than eight divisions, and I have not thought it necessary to mention all of them, omitting some which are of smaller importance.

1. Philosophical

386 Against the Academics—3 books.
On a Happy Life.
On Order.
387 On the Immortality of the Soul.
On the 'Quantity' of the Soul.
389 On Music—8 books.

These books are of quite subordinate importance. They were written after his conversion, but before, or immediately after, his baptism, and are still largely dominated by Platonic conceptions.

2. Apologetic

To this class belongs his best work.

> On the City of God—22 books.
> This treatise, of which I have already spoken, was begun in 413, but not completed till 426, when he was 72 years old.

3. Polemic

a. Against the Manicheans

388   On the Morals of the Manicheans.
391   On the Usefulness of Believing.
392   On the Two Souls.
> The Manicheans believed that there were two souls, one of which was a part of God, and the other from the race of darkness.

> Against Adimantus.
397   Against the Epistle of 'the Foundation'.
> Against the Letter of a Manichee.
404   Against Faustus—33 books.
> Against Felix—2 books.
> On the Nature of the Good.
> Against Secundinus.
> Against Fortunatus.

b. Against the Donatists

393   An Alphabetical Psalm Against the Donatists.
> Against the Letter of Donatus.
400   Against the Letter of Parmenian—4 books.
> On Baptism—7 books.
> Against the Letter of Petilian—3 books.
402   On the Unity of the Church.
406   To the Grammarian Cresconius—4 books.
> On One Baptism.
411   The Conference with the Donatists—3 books.
> After the Conference.
417   On the Correction of the Donatists.
420   Against Gaudentius.

c. Against the Pelagians

410   On the Deserts of Sin, and on Remission—3 books.
       On Marriage and Concupiscence—2 books.
       Against Semi-Pelagians.
413   On the Spirit and the Letter.
415   On Nature and Grace.
       On the Doings of Pelagius.
       On the Presence of God.
422   To Valentius, on Grace and Free-Will.
427   On Grace.
       Against Gaudentius—2 books.
       Against Two Letters—4 books.
428   On Predestination.
       On the Gift of Perseverance.
       Against Pelagius and Coelestius.
       Doings with Emeritus.
429   Against Julian—6 books.

d. Against the Heathen

410   Questions Explained Against the Pagans.

e. Against the Priscillianists and Origenists

411   To Orosius.

f. Against the Arians

416   On the Trinity—15 books.
       Against a Sermon of the Arians.
428   Conference with the Arian Maximin.
       Against the Arians.
       Against Maximin—2 books.

g. Against the Marcionists

420   Against an Enemy of the Law and the Prophets.

4. Dogmatic

389 On the Master (Matthew 23:10).

390 On True Religion.
In this book he had said that in his day miracles had ceased. This he retracts, in consequence of the miracles wrought by the relics of Gervasius and Protasius, especially a blind man's recovery of sight.
On the Spirit and the Letter.
On Seeing God.

393 On Faith and the Creed.

395 On Free-Will.

400 On Catechising the Uninstructed.
It is addressed to a young deacon.

408 On the Grace of Christ.

410 On the Soul and its Origin—4 books.

413 On Faith and Works.

416 On the Trinity—15 books.
Augustine begins this book with the remark that it is difficult, and will be understood by few, in consequence of its highly speculative character.

420 Enchiridion; or, on Faith, Hope, and Love.
To the Enquiries of Januarius—2 books.

421 On the Care for the Dead.
This book was addressed to Paulinus. It contains one of the earliest authoritative statements of the belief in an intermediate state between blessedness and damnation, and in the benefit to be gained from the prayers of the faithful by those in this condition.
On the Grace of the New Testament.
On the Divination of Demons.
On the Origin of the Soul and a Text of James —2 books.

426 On Christian Doctrine—4 books.
This important work is a sort of sketch of hermeneutics and homiletics, and may be regarded as an introduction to Augustine's Commentaries.

429 On Heresies, to Quodvultdeus.

5. Moral and Ascetic

390 On Lying.
He was not at all pleased with this book, and at one time tried to suppress it.

395 On Continence.

396 On the Christian Contest.

396 On the Christian Warfare.

397 On Virginity.

400 On the Work of Monks.
A censure of idle and vagabond monks and relic-mongers.

401 On the Blessing of Marriage.

411 On Consulting Demons.

414 On the Blessing of Widowhood.

418 On Abstinence.
On Patience.

419 On Adulterous Unions.

420 Against Lying.
In these books Augustine shows himself superior to the general moral standpoint of the age by arguing against the view of the Priscillianists that a falsehood is not allowable under any circumstances, and not even to our worst enemies, or for a supposed good purpose.

6. Exegetical

393 On Eighty-three Questions.
Questions on the Gospel—2 books.
On the Sermon on the Mount—2 books.
On Parts of the Epistle to the Romans.

394 On the Epistle to the Galatians.

397 On Different Questions. To Simplicianus
—3 books.

400 On the Agreement of the Evangelists—4 books.

401–405 On Genesis, taken literally—12 books.

410 On the Psalms.
On Job.
On Forms of Expression in the Scriptures—7 books.

Questions—7 books.

412   On the Spirit and the Letter.

416   On the Gospel of St John—124 homilies.
Begun 406.

417   Homilies on the First Epistle of St John.

We have already had occasion to notice some of the characteristics of Augustine's exegesis. He held, but in a loose and elastic way, the doctrine of the 'plenary inspiration' of scripture, yet he points out that it was possible for the meritorious to do without scripture altogether, and says that when men are upheld by faith, hope, and charity, they only need scripture for the instruction of others.

7. Sermons, *circa* 400

They are homilies, of which 183 are on passages of scripture, 88 on festivals, 69 on saints, 23 on occasional subjects. Admirably adapted for their immediate purposes, often interesting, and never without some marks of the ability of the preacher, they are yet the least important division of Augustine's writings. Many of them were published from the notes of shorthand reports of his hearers. They do not for a moment pretend to be great and deep orations like the masterpieces of the Greek Fathers, but are models of country sermons addressed to the middle classes and the poor of Hippo in a terse and simple style.

8. Autobiographical

Letters.
These are 270 in number, and are spread over a space of forty years. They furnish us with a vivid picture, both of Augustine himself and of the times in which he lived. They are addressed to bishops, clerics of all ranks, statesmen, ladies, and private friends, and they range over all the public and private events of his day. They abound in points of interest. For instance, in the 22nd he begs the Bishop of Carthage to forbid the revels at wakes and at

the tombs of the martyrs. Of the correspondence with Jerome I have already spoken. In the 38th he pleads for some allowance in ritual diversities. The 47th deals with justifiable homicides. The 53rd gives the succession of the Bishops of Rome, from St Peter to Anastasius. In the 54th he touches on a question now frequently discussed. He tells us that the Holy Communion was received fasting, yet that on the eve of Good Friday it was not so received, and he does not venture to lay down such a rule. The Church of England 'has so ordered her services that the Holy Communion is commonly administered at noon', and Augustine's rule was, 'Whatsoever cannot be shown to be contrary to the faith or to good morals is to be regarded as indifferent.' The 54th is on the mysteries of numbers. The 60th is on the character produced by monasticism. The 65th, 77th, and 78th are on criminous clerks. The 90th is on heaven and the heavenly life on earth. In the 93rd Epistle occurs the sophistical plea of the Inquisition. In the 98th Epistle he repudiates the notion of any continuation or repetition of Christian sacrifice, in spite of the popular phrase, 'the sacrifice of the altar'. In the 101st letter he confesses his ignorance of Hebrew. The 146th is memorable as being addressed 'to the delectable doctor and most desirable brother', namely to Pelagius! In the 149th he explains Colossians 2:18–23, and refers, as he rarely does, to the Greek text and its divergent readings. In the 157th he dwells on the lawfulness of divorce for fornication and infidelity, and severely reprobates the monastic *disparagements* of marriage. In the 159th he makes some remarks on the appearance of ghosts. In the 165th and 166th he shows his leaning to the doctrine of *traducianism* (as also in letters 180, 202), though he appeals to Jerome for his opinion. He also speaks of the punishment of infants dying unbaptised. In the 169th he speaks of Christ as the rock on which the church is built. The 189th is on the lawfulness of war. In the 197th and 199th, 'On the End of the World', he expresses opinions which practically seem to exclude the doctrines of purgatory and prayers for the dead. The 204th is on suicide. The 209th is on the appointment of a suffragan. His choice of a monk named Antony was so unhappy that it caused him the acutest distress, and almost drove him to resign his see. Augustine superseded him, and wrote to Pope Caelestine not to accept his appeal. The 211th deals with the disorder of a sisterhood. The 213th is about the appointment of a successor. The 220th is a reproof to Count Boniface. The 228th is on flight in persecution. The last is addressed to Count Darius, with a copy of his *Confessions*.

387   Soliloquies.

400   Confessions—13 books.

Of this most remarkable and all but unique work I have already spoken. It has been better known in all ages and to all classes of readers than any other of his voluminous writings.

427   Retractations—2 books.

This work also is of an unusual and interesting character. About the year 427, when Augustine had already reached the limit of old age, it occurred to him to revise his own books with something of a judicial severity. He had been a very prolific writer, and, thinking of the words of St Paul, 'if we judged ourselves, we would not come under judgment' (1 Corinthians 11:31), he admitted that he was afraid of the warnings against 'every careless word' (Matthew 12:36), and also of the text: 'When words are many, sin is not absent' (Proverbs 10:19). He was well aware that from his many treatises many things could be collected, which, if not false, could yet certainly be proved to be unnecessary. He does not apply these remarks to his sermons. He had begun to speak to the people while he was yet young and had rarely been permitted to be silent on any public occasion. He therefore passes in review his principal works. In his books against the Academics he regrets that he has so often spoken of 'fortune', and that he had used the word 'omen', which he does not find in the sacred writings. He thinks, too, that he should not have praised Plato and his followers so highly, seeing that they were pagans. In the dedication of his treatise *On a Happy Life* to Manlius Theodorus he had been too complimentary. In his book *On Order* he had attached too high an importance to a liberal education, since many who had no such education were great saints, and many who had greatly advanced in it were not saints at all. Also he should not have spoken of the Muses as though they were goddesses, nor have spoken of wonder as a vice, nor have spoken of the philosophers as illustrious for virtue, though they had not true piety. His book *On the Immortality of the Soul* was so brief and obscure that in some places he could not even understand it himself. As to others of his books, he is obliged to enter into subtle, and not always very satisfactory, explanations, to show that they cannot be quoted by the Pelagians in favour of their views about free-will. Yet, on the whole, the *Retractations* are a noble sacrifice laid on the altar of truth by a majestic intellect.